Hello and welcome!

*Vor dir liegt der **Wordmaster**. Er hilft dir beim Wörterlernen.*

*Sobald du neue Wörter in der Schule besprochen hast, mach die **New words and phrases** in diesem Heft.*

*Die **fett gedruckten** deutschen Wörter sind Lernwörter. Sie fehlen im englischen Satz, damit du sie eintragen kannst.*

*Im Anschluss an die **New words and phrases** gibt es kurze Aufgaben, Rätsel und Wortspiele, mit denen du den neuen Wortschatz übst und festigst.*

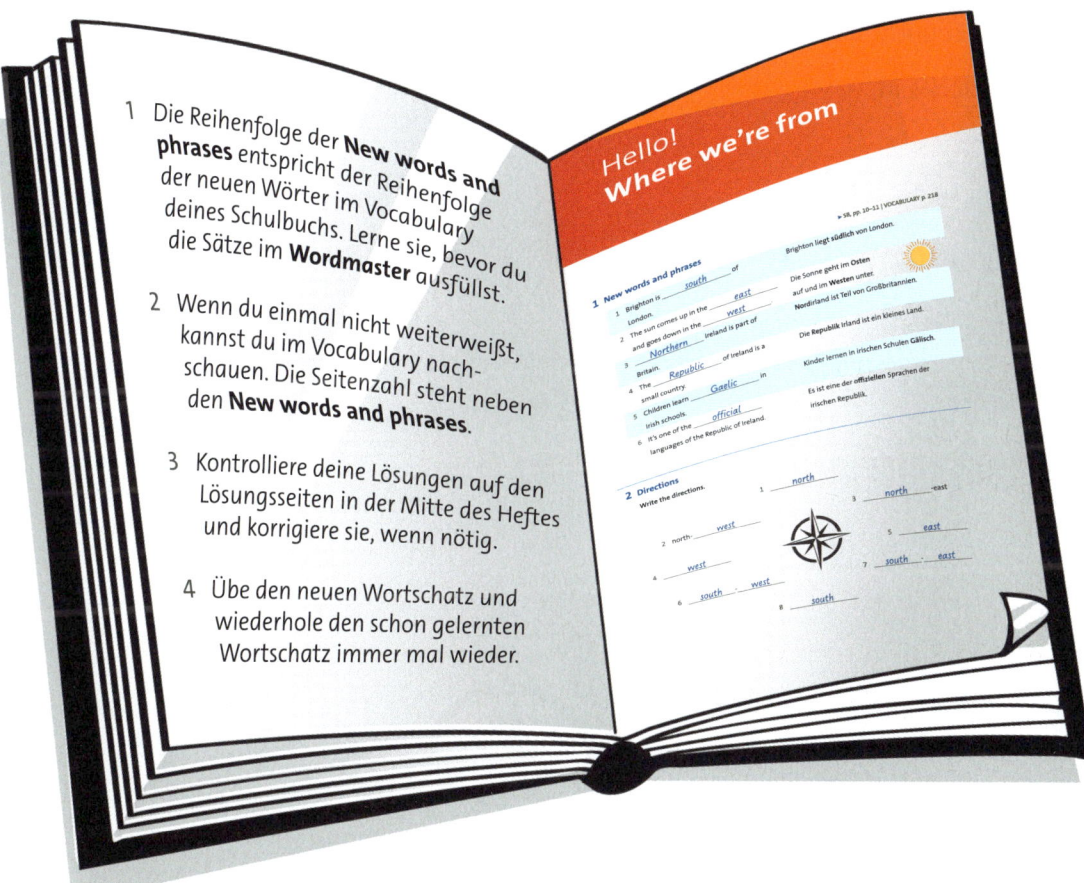

1 Die Reihenfolge der **New words and phrases** entspricht der Reihenfolge der neuen Wörter im Vocabulary deines Schulbuchs. Lerne sie, bevor du die Sätze im **Wordmaster** ausfüllst.

2 Wenn du einmal nicht weiterweißt, kannst du im Vocabulary nachschauen. Die Seitenzahl steht neben den **New words and phrases**.

3 Kontrolliere deine Lösungen auf den Lösungsseiten in der Mitte des Heftes und korrigiere sie, wenn nötig.

4 Übe den neuen Wortschatz und wiederhole den schon gelernten Wortschatz immer mal wieder.

Alle Lösungen findest du auf den Lösungsseiten in der Mitte des Heftes. Die Hörtexte 🔊 zu den Listen carefully!-Aufgaben kannst du in deiner Cornelsen Lernen App aufrufen. Dort findest du auch noch einmal die Lösungen.

Hello!
Where we're from

1 New words and phrases

▶ SB, pp. 10–11 | VOCABULARY p. 218

1 Brighton is _____ of London.

Brighton liegt **südlich** von London.

2 The sun comes up in the _____ and goes down in the _____.

Die Sonne geht im **Osten** auf und im **Westen** unter.

3 _____ Ireland is part of Britain.

Nordirland ist Teil von Großbritannien.

4 The _____ of Ireland is a small country.

Die **Republik** Irland ist ein kleines Land.

5 Children learn _____ in Irish schools.

Kinder lernen in irischen Schulen **Gälisch**.

6 It's one of the _____ languages of the Republic of Ireland.

Es ist eine der **offiziellen** Sprachen der irischen Republik.

2 Directions

Write the directions.

1 _____

2 north-_____

3 _____-east

4 _____

5 _____

6 _____-_____

7 _____-_____

8 _____

▶ Check

3 New words and phrases

▶ SB, pp. 12–13 | VOCABULARY pp. 218–219

1 It's hard to learn how to play the _____.

Es ist schwer zu lernen, **Dudelsack** zu spielen.

2 We walked around the _____.

Wir sind um den **See** gelaufen.

3 My mum works in a _____ in the city.

Meine Mutter arbeitet in einem **Wolkenkratzer** in der Stadt.

4 On one side of the building there is a big beautiful _____.

Auf einer Seite des Gebäudes befindet sich ein großes, wunderschönes **Wandgemälde**.

5 My uncle bought a _____ because he loves the sea.

Mein Onkel hat ein **Boot** gekauft, weil er das Meer liebt.

6 The ship was too big for the _____.

Das Schiff war zu groß für den **Kanal**.

7 In the photo there's a girl in the _____ and the city of London in the _____.

Auf dem Foto ist im **Vordergrund** ein Mädchen und im **Hintergrund** die Stadt London zu sehen.

8 Germany is part of the _____ _____.

Deutschland ist Teil der **Europäischen Union**.

9 The _____ was yesterday. It was very _____ but I won!

Die **Abstimmung** war gestern. Es war sehr **knapp**, aber ich habe gewonnen!

10 Where's the _____?

Wo ist der **Ausgang**?

11 Try some of our _____ dishes.

Probieren Sie einige unserer **regionalen** Gerichte.

12 My parents want to _____ in this _____.

Meine Eltern wollen in dieser **Gegend bleiben**.

4 Odd word out

Underline the word that doesn't go with the other words.

1 song – music – bagpipes – talk

2 lake – sea – swim – canal

3 street – skyscraper – bridge – tunnel

4 picture – photo – mural – story

5 boat – bus – bike – car

6 middle – foreground – underground – background

5 Listen carefully!

Listen carefully to the sentences and write the right word in each gap.

1 My friend lives in the _____ part of the country.

2 I love the sound of the _____ language.

3 Please leave through the _____ at the back of the room.

4 The country became a _____ in 2012.

5 My country has four _____ languages.

6 The artist painted a beautiful _____ .

7 There are three boats in the _____ today.

8 My mother is the woman in the _____ of the photo.

9 The vote was very _____ .

10 He asked me to _____ the door.

6 Definitions

Read the definitions and write the words in the boxes. The solution is in the blue boxes.

1 near *or* nearly the same

2 You paint this large picture on a wall.

3 to stay

4 from a certain area

5 Ireland is this kind of country.

6 People have one of these to pick a person for an important job or to decide something.

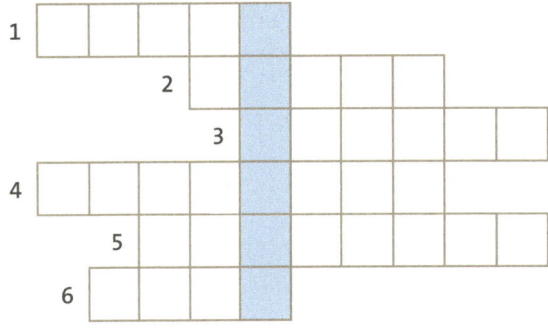

Solution: _____

► Check

Unit 1
London: City life

1 New words and phrases

▶SB, pp. 14–15 | VOCABULARY pp. 219–220

1 Every day, four _____ do a show.   Jeden Tag treten vier **Akrobaten/**

Akrobatinnen auf.

2 The British _____ has two houses.   Das britische **Parlament** hat zwei Kammern.

3 I like the _____ in this park.   Ich mag die **Skulptur** in diesem Park.

4 The _____ is higher than my house!   Die **Rutsche** ist höher als mein Haus! Die

The children love to _____ on it.   Kinder lieben es, darauf zu **rutschen**.

5 I wasn't scared in the dark _____.   Ich hatte im dunklen **Tunnel** keine Angst.

6 The _____ was really exciting.   Die **Fahrt** war wirklich aufregend.

7 Why does your car only have three   Warum hat Ihr Auto nur drei **Räder**?

_____?

8 The boat leaves from the south   Das Boot fährt vom Süd**ufer** des Flusses ab.

_____ of the river.

9 You can buy apples at this _____.   Du kannst an diesem **Stand** Äpfel kaufen.

2 Silhouettes

Write the names of the things.

_____   _____

_____

_____   _____

_____

3 New words and phrases

▶ SB, p. 16 | VOCABULARY pp. 220–221

1 Max bought the T-shirt _____ the colour.

Max hat das T-Shirt **wegen** der Farbe gekauft.

2 The _____ in the city was terrible today so I _____ to walk.

Der **Verkehr** in der Stadt war schrecklich heute, darum **beschloss** ich, zu Fuß zu gehen.

3 Ann uses a London _____ for the bus.

Für den Bus nutzt Ann eine Londoner **Mehrtagesfahrkarte**.

4 The _____ in the stations are really long!

Die **Rolltreppen** in den Bahnhöfen sind wirklich lang!

5 Lou takes the _____ to school.

Lou fährt mit der (Londoner) **U-Bahn** zur Schule.

6 There's no _____ in this station.

In diesem Bahnhof gibt es kein **WLAN**.

7 _____ your bag in the city.

Achten Sie auf Ihre Tasche in der Stadt.

8 Careful! There's a _____ between the train and the platform.

Vorsicht! Es gibt eine **Lücke** zwischen dem Zug und dem Bahnsteig.

9 This is not a _____ park!

Dies ist kein **öffentlicher** Park!

10 The _____ schools are very good.

Die Schulen **am Ort** sind sehr gut.

11 Is the _____ always late?

Kommt die **Straßenbahn** immer zu spät?

4 New words and phrases

▶ SB, pp. 17–18 | VOCABULARY p. 221

1 _____ me go first, please.

Lass mich bitte zuerst gehen.

2 It's easier to take the _____ .

Es ist einfacher, mit dem **Aufzug** zu fahren.

3 Can you _____ this thing?

Kannst du dieses Ding **heben**?

4 This is a _____ train.

Dies ist ein **Direkt**zug.

5 Janie gave me an _____ answer.

Janie gab mir eine **indirekte** Antwort.

6 This _____ doesn't go to the airport.

Diese **Linie** fährt nicht zum Flughafen.

7 Good evening, _____ _____ .

Guten Abend, **sehr geehrte Damen und Herren**.

8 _____ your rubbish in the bin, please.

Bitte **werfen** Sie Ihren Müll in den Mülleimer.

▶ Check

5 New words and phrases

▶ SB, p. 19 | VOCABULARY pp. 221–222

1 There are _____ 700 students in my school.

Es gibt **ungefähr** 700 Schüler und Schülerinnen an meiner Schule.

2 Our country has spent _____ on this new project.

Unser Land hat **Milliarden** für dieses neue Projekt ausgegeben.

3 _____ of people _____ saw this film loved it.

Millionen von Menschen, **die** den Film sahen, liebten ihn.

4 We _____ missed our train yesterday.

Wir haben gestern unseren Zug **fast** verpasst.

5 Sorry, but our computer _____ isn't working today.

Sorry, aber unser Computer**system** funktioniert heute nicht.

6 There isn't any _____ between here and London.

Es gibt keine **Bahnverbindung** zwischen hier und London.

7 I'm very tired today. I'm seeing _____.

Ich bin heute sehr müde. Ich sehe alles **doppelt**.

8 You can see a lot from a _____.

Von einem **Doppeldeckerbus** aus kann man viel sehen.

9 We have a big _____ in our hotel.

Wir haben ein großes **Doppelzimmer** in unserem Hotel.

10 The car isn't big enough for all of our _____.

Das Auto ist nicht groß genug für unser ganzes **Gepäck**.

11 It's expensive to take a _____.

Es ist teuer, ein **Taxi** zu nehmen.

12 You must _____ before you can do this job.

Du musst **einen Test machen**, bevor du diesen Job ausüben darfst.

13 You can _____ a bike for the day.

Sie können für den Tag ein Fahrrad **mieten**.

14 Look right when you _____ the road in England.

Schau nach rechts, wenn du in England die Straße **überquerst**.

15 I marked the museum with a _____ on the map.

Ich habe das Museum auf der Karte mit einem **Kreuz** markiert.

6 The right verb

Complete each sentence with the right verb. Careful: There are two extra verbs!

> (to) cross • (to) decide • (to) hire • (to) let • (to) lift • (to) mind •
> (to) slide • (to) take a test • (to) throw

1 Our class will _____ in history tomorrow.

2 Can someone please _____ the ball to me?

3 Don't _____ the street here: It's too dangerous.

4 Ice cream or cake? I can't _____!

5 My parents won't _____ me go to England alone.

6 I want to _____ on the Orbit!

7 Dana helped me to _____ my luggage onto the train.

7 Definitions

Tick the right word for each definition.

1	maybe a few more or less than ...	under	☐	about	☐	above	☐
2	a kind of box that takes you up and down in a building	lift	☐	rail	☐	escalator	☐
3	lots of different parts make up one of these	traffic	☐	public	☐	system	☐
4	1,000,000	billion	☐	thousand	☐	million	☐
5	to pay attention to; to be careful of	(to) worry	☐	(to) mind	☐	(to) decide	☐
6	the big bags you take on a trip	clothes	☐	luggage	☐	furniture	☐
7	1,000,000,000	billion	☐	hundred	☐	million	☐
8	train(s)	bus	☐	line	☐	rail	☐

▶ Check

8 New words and phrases

▶ SB, p. 20 | VOCABULARY pp. 222–223

1   Riding my bike is my favourite _____ of transport.

Fahrradfahren ist meine Lieblings**art** der Fortbewegung.

2   The price _____ all meals.

Der Preis **schließt** alle Mahlzeiten mit **ein**.

3   We visited several countries in the holidays, _____ England.

Wir besuchten in den Ferien mehrere Länder, **einschließlich** England.

4   The tour went to eight cool _____.

Die Tour führte zu acht coolen **Orten**.

5   Zoe lost her _____ ring.

Zoe verlor ihren **goldenen** Ring.

6   Our new teacher is very _____.

Unsere neue Lehrerin ist sehr **jung**.

7   The _____ has fourteen horses.

Der **Prinz** hat vierzehn Pferde.

8   Where does the _____ family live?

Wo lebt die **königliche** Familie?

9   _____ Charles was born in 1948.

König Charles wurde 1948 geboren.

10   The _____ never wears dresses.

Die **Königin** trägt nie Kleider.

11   The _____ lost her shoe.

Die **Prinzessin** verlor ihren Schuh.

12   My mother doesn't like the _____ tourist activities.

Meine Mutter mag die **klassischen** Touristenaktivitäten nicht.

13   I didn't vote for this _____ _____.

Ich habe diese **Premierministerin** nicht gewählt.

14   We saw everything _____ the museum.

Wir haben alles gesehen **bis auf** das Museum.

15   Is it _____ to meet the king today?

Ist es **möglich**, den König heute zu treffen?

9 Lost letters

Complete the words with the missing letters.

1 B__ c __ __ s __ of all the 2 t__ __ f __ __ c in London, the fastest way to get to my house is with the 3 __ __ b __. There's a 4 __ __ r __ct 5 l__ __ __ from the airport to our station. You can buy a 6 T__ __ v __ __ c __ __ __ for the week. When you get to our station, take the 7 __ __ f __ up to the street level: It's hard to take a lot of 8 l__ g __ __ __ __ __ on the 9 __ sc __ __ __ __ __r.

10 New words and phrases

▶SB, p. 21 | VOCABULARY p. 223

1. _____ your bike across the street.   **Schiebe** dein Rad über die Straße.

2. A rude girl gave me a strong _____.   Ein freches Mädchen gab mir einen kräftigen **Stoß**.

3. She used the _____ to close the door.   Sie benutzte den **Griff**, um die Tür zu schließen.

4. Under what _____ can we change our travel plans?   Unter welchen **Bedingungen** können wir unsere Reisepläne ändern?

11 That's what will happen!

Complete each sentence with a word from the box. Careful: There are three extra words!

> bank • billion • gap • (to) hire • local • (to) mind • parliament •
> prime minister • prince • (to) push • site • tram

1. If he wins the vote, he'll be in the _____.

2. The people will want a new _____ if this one isn't good.

3. She'll _____ a bike if she doesn't want to walk.

4. If you want to visit that _____, you'll need to buy a ticket.

5. He'll have an accident if he doesn't _____ the traffic.

6. If I _____ him, he'll be really angry.

7. If we take the _____ train, we'll be late.

8. If I win a _____ pounds, I'll buy you a new car!

9. If your phone falls into the _____, you won't get it back.

▶ Check

12 New words and phrases

▶ SB, p. 22 | VOCABULARY p. 223

1 Don't forget to _____ the guide after the tour! She only earns money from _____.

Vergessen Sie nicht, der Reiseleiterin nach der Führung **Trinkgeld** zu **geben**. Sie verdient nur durch **Trinkgelder**.

2 He's from _____ Petersburg.

Er kommt aus **Sankt** Petersburg.

3 This hotel is great: _____ but quiet!

Dieses Hotel ist großartig: **zentral**, aber ruhig.

4 That _____ is eating a big fish.

Der **Pelikan** isst gerade einen großen Fisch.

5 Is that fruit _____?

Ist das Obst **frisch**?

13 New words and phrases

▶ SB, p. 23 | VOCABULARY pp. 223–224

1 I took a _____ tour of London.

Ich habe eine **virtuelle** Tour durch London gemacht.

2 Cars drive on the left side of the _____ in England.

Autos fahren in England auf der linken **Straßen**seite.

3 There's a sculpture in the middle of the _____.

In der Mitte des **Kreisverkehrs** steht eine Skulptur.

4 The sculpture stands on a _____.

Die Skulptur steht auf einer **Säule**.

5 There are _____ in front of the palace. They _____ the King.

Vor dem Palast stehen **Wachen**. Sie **schützen** den König.

6 You can hire your own _____ on the London Eye, but it's not cheap.

Man kann am London Eye eine eigene **Kabine** mieten, aber es ist nicht billig.

7 If you walk _____ _____, you'll see the London Eye.

Wenn man **die Straße entlang**geht, sieht man schon das London Eye.

14 New words and phrases

▶ SB, pp. 24–25 | VOCABULARY pp. 224–225

1   This new organization finds flats for
    _____ people.

    Diese neue Organisation vermittelt Wohnungen für **obdachlose** Menschen.

2   I liked the _____
    park, and the _____
    flowers were beautiful!

    Ich mochte den **friedlichen** Park, und die **bunten** Blumen waren wunderschön!

3   I'm ill, so please go to the game
    _____ me.

    Ich bin krank, also geh bitte **ohne** mich zum Spiel.

4   He cleaned the sculpture with great
    _____.

    Er hat die Skulptur mit großer **Sorgfalt** gereinigt.

5   Ron _____ for the
    neighbours' kids every day after school.

    Ron **passt** jeden Tag nach der Schule auf die Kinder der Nachbarn **auf**.

6   Sally's _____ is to run
    10 miles.

    Sallys **Ziel** ist es, 10 Meilen zu laufen.

7   The city's plans for the future aren't really
    _____.

    Die Zukunftspläne der Stadt sind nicht wirklich **nachhaltig**.

8   Emily likes to help her
    _____.

    Emily hilft gerne ihrer **Gemeinde**.

9   I have _____ stress
    today than yesterday.

    Ich habe heute **weniger** Stress als gestern.

10 There are very _____
    sights in my town.

    Es gibt sehr **wenige** Sehenswürdigkeiten in meiner Stadt.

11 There was _____
    milk in the bottle and I drank it all!

    Es war **wenig** Milch in der Flasche und ich hab sie aufgetrunken.

12 Lots of cities have _____
    _____ now.

    Viele Städte haben inzwischen **Radwege**.

13 There's a lot of _____
    _____ in the city.

    Es gibt viel **Luftverschmutzung** in der Stadt.

14 Sophie wants to _____
    a tour of London this summer.

    Sophie möchte im Sommer eine Tour durch London **leiten**.

15 We'll _____ her
    _____ of our group.

    Wir werden sie **zur Leiterin** unserer Gruppe **machen**.

▶ Check

🔊 15 Listen carefully!
02

Listen carefully to the sentences and write the right word in each gap.

1 The newspaper has five _____ on each page.

2 Our hotel stands on the _____ of an old theatre.

3 We saw all of the museum _____ the top floor.

4 Did you _____ what to do today?

5 You can take the lift or the _____ down to the platform.

6 I booked a _____ room in the hotel.

7 There was a _____ at the bank.

8 Alex went up on the big _____ but he didn't like it.

9 We fed the _____ in our _____ park.

10 Walking is a very _____ form of transport.

16 Groups of three

What word goes with each group? Write the right word from the box. You can use each word only once.

| air • cab • homeless • less • pollution • road |

1 rubbish   dirty   _____

2 poor   street   _____

3 tube   tram   _____

4 smaller   fewer   _____

5 water   land   _____

6 street   lane   _____

17 Rhyming words

Underline the word that doesn't rhyme with the other three words in each line.

1 ride – bridge – slide – guide

2 care – air – hear – wear

3 site – eight – write – right

4 wheel – meal – health – real

18 New words and phrases

▶SB, pp. 26–27 | VOCABULARY p. 226

1   Turn on the _____, please.

Dreh bitte den **Wasserhahn** auf.

2   We don't like _____ so we

bought a bottle of _____ water.

Wir mögen kein **Leitungswasser**, deshalb

kauften wir eine Flasche **Sprudel**wasser.

3   This blanket is very _____.

Diese Decke ist sehr **weich**.

4   They will only serve _____ at

the party.

Sie werden auf der Feier nur **alkoholfreie**

Getränke servieren.

5   The food came with a _____ sauce.

Zum Essen gab es eine **Minz**soße.

6   Eve put five _____ on the table.

Eve stellte fünf **Teller** auf den Tisch.

7   Joe hates _____.

Joe hasst **Auberginen.**

8   Have you ever tried _____

soup? It's really good!

Hast du schon einmal **Gurken**suppe

probiert? Sie ist sehr lecker!

9   I like green _____,

not black ones.

Ich mag grüne **Oliven**, keine

schwarzen.

10 Try the _____ bread.

Probiere mal das

Sesambrot.

11 _____ a salad and some tea.

Ich nehme einen Salat und einen Tee.

12 You _____ the food an hour

ago! Ask our _____ why it's

taking so long. Or ask the _____

in the blue shirt.

Du **hast** das Essen vor einer Stunde **bestellt!**

Frag unseren **Kellner**, warum es so lange

dauert. Oder frag die **Kellnerin** im blauen

Hemd.

13 Our teacher is going to _____

a new student to our class.

Unser Lehrer wird unserer Klasse einen

neuen Schüler **vorstellen.**

14 It's important to start a newspaper article with a

short _____.

Es ist wichtig, einen Zeitungsartikel mit

einer kurzen **Einleitung** zu beginnen.

15 Read the first _____ and then

answer the questions.

Lies den ersten **Abschnitt** und beantworte

dann die Fragen.

▶ Check

19 New words and phrases

▶ SB, pp. 28–30 | VOCABULARY pp. 226–228

1 These are _____ of famous people.

Dies sind **Statuen** berühmter Personen.

2 Ana always goes home _____ _____.

Ana geht immer **gleich nach der Schule** nach Hause.

3 Our hotel is very small and it doesn't have a _____.

Unser Hotel ist sehr klein und hat keine/n **Pförtner/in**.

4 My hands always _____ before a presentation.

Mir **zittern** immer die Hände vor einer Präsentation.

5 Luisa _____ her head sadly in answer.

Luisa **schüttelte** traurig den Kopf als Antwort.

6 Walk _____ Big Ben.

Gehen Sie **in Richtung** Big Ben.

7 I love your curls. Are they _____?

Ich liebe deine Locken. Sind sie **natürlich**?

8 The cows ate all the _____.

Die Kühe haben das ganze **Gras** gefressen.

9 "I have two hours of homework," _____ Angie.

„Ich habe zwei Stunden Hausaufgaben", **seufzte** Angie.

10 We _____ to the bus.

Wir **eilten** zum Bus.

11 Can you please tell me the best _____ to the park?

Kannst du mir bitte die beste **Route** zum Park nennen?

12 I've looked at all the _____ but I still haven't found the solution.

Ich habe mir alle **Hinweise** angesehen, aber die Lösung immer noch nicht gefunden.

13 The _____ leads to the lake.

Der **Weg** führt zum See.

14 Ezra likes to eat his lunch on a _____ in the park.

Ezra isst sein Mittagessen gerne auf einer **Bank** im Park.

15 I don't know where I am. All the streets look _____!

Ich weiß nicht, wo ich bin. Die Straßen sehen alle **ähnlich** aus!

20 New words and phrases

▶ SB, p. 31 | VOCABULARY p. 228

1 Emily _____ at the park every weekend.

Emily **arbeitet** jedes Wochenende **ehrenamtlich** im Park.

2 Paul is a _____ at the hospital.

Paul ist **ehrenamtlicher Mitarbeiter** im Krankenhaus.

3 I didn't _____ you with short hair!

Ich habe dich mit den kurzen Haaren nicht **erkannt!**

4 Learning vocabulary really _____ _____ in your marks!

Vokabeln lernen **macht** bei den Noten wirklich **etwas aus**!

21 Categories

Write three words from the box for each category.

aubergine • bench • cab • cucumber • grass • king • olive • prince • queen • statue • tram • tube

1 Things in a park: _____ _____ _____

2 Foods: _____ _____ _____

3 Things to ride in: _____ _____ _____

4 People in the royal family: _____ _____ _____

22 Word families

Write a word from the same word family in each gap. Careful: Some of the words have the same form!

	noun	verb	adjective
1	mind	*(to) mind*	mindful
2		(to) air	airy
3		(to) pollute	polluted
4	sparkle	(to) sparkle	
5			introductory
6	opposition	(to) oppose	
7			volunteer
8	public	(to) publicize	

▶ Check

23 New words and phrases

▶ SB, pp. 32–33 | VOCABULARY pp. 228–229

1 I _____ everywhere for my phone.

Ich **suchte** überall nach meinem Handy.

2 The most _____ photo of Oscar is two years old.

Das **aktuellste** Foto von Oscar ist zwei Jahre alt.

3 My family was _____ in London.

Meine Familie war **kürzlich** in London.

4 They work for the _____.

Sie arbeiten für die **Regierung**.

5 Alison's _____ makes computers and phones.

Alisons **Firma** stellt Computer und Telefone her.

6 It's cool how they use _____ to make these _____.

Es ist cool, wie sie **Wachs** verwenden, um diese **Figuren** herzustellen.

7 Our club has _____ weekly meetings.

Unser Club trifft sich **regelmäßig** jede Woche.

8 Can you please _____ this text?

Kannst du bitte diesen Text **kopieren**?

9 My parents used a travel _____ to plan our holiday.

Meine Eltern nutzten eine Reise**agentur**, um unseren Urlaub zu planen.

10 Logan has a very soft _____.

Logan hat eine sehr leise **Stimme**.

24 Listen carefully!

03

Listen carefully to the sentences and write the right word in each gap.

1 Can you please put some _____ and the _____ on the table?

2 This _____ looks very _____ to one in London.

3 My salad has a lot of _____ in it.

4 The first _____ of the article _____ the topic.

5 The _____ figures don't have _____.

6 Everyone looked _____ the lights.

7 Please call the _____ tomorrow.

25 Verb walk

Walk along the old London street, but only on the stones with verbs in the simple past!
Draw a line from one stone to the next.

26 Opposites

Write the opposite words.

1 different ◀▶ _____
2 hard ◀▶ _____
3 possible ◀▶ _____
4 more ◀▶ _____
5 many ◀▶ _____

6 with ◀▶ _____
7 indirect ◀▶ _____
8 old ◀▶ _____
9 ladies ◀▶ _____
10 a long time ago ◀▶ _____

27 Giving directions

Give directions from Buckingham Palace to the London Eye. Use the words from the box.

across • along • bridge • left (2x) • past • right • river • see • straight • turn

Go 1 _____ this street and then 2 _____ left. Go 3 _____ on,

4 _____ the park. Then you'll 5 _____ Big Ben on your 6 _____ . The

London Eye is 7 _____ the river on the 8 _____ . Go across the

9 _____ . Take the path on the 10 _____ and follow the 11 _____ .

You'll see the ticket office and a lot of people!

28 Let's talk: Essen gehen und in einem Restaurant bestellen

▶ SB, p. 209

Use the menu to order something to eat and drink.

Lighthouse (General Edition) Band 3 (9783060365425), S. 24

★ Menu ★

Drinks

| 1 | Tap water | free | 3 | Soft drinks | £1.90 | 5 | Mint tea | £2.00 |
| 2 | Sparkling water | £1.50 | 4 | Mango milkshake | £2.60 | 6 | Coffee | £2.30 |

Lebanese small plates

7	Hummus (chickpea dip)	£5.75
8	Halloumi cheese with cucumber and olives	£6.25
9	Kibbeh (lamb meatballs)	£6.50
10	Spicy sausages with lemon	£6.50
11	Falafel with sesame sauce	£6.25
12	Chicken with spicy potatoes	£7.50
13	Bread	90p

Good evening! What would you like to eat?

_____
_____

Do you have any food allergies?

Yes, I'm allergic to _____ . /

No, _____ .

OK, thanks! Your food comes with soup or salad. Which would you like?

_____
_____

Can I bring you anything to drink?

Yes, _____ .

I'll be back with your food in a few minutes.

_____

Unit 2
Manchester: Who we are

1 New words and phrases
▶ SB, pp. 48–49 | VOCABULARY p. 229

1	Brett isn't interested in _____.	Brett interessiert sich nicht für **Mode**.
2	Fred's _____ on a hard day was very important to me.	Freds **Freundlichkeit** an einem harten Tag hat mir viel bedeutet.
3	Lux has a _____. It makes it hard for her to walk.	Lux hat eine **Behinderung**. Sie erschwert ihr das Gehen.
4	These seats are for _____ people.	Diese Plätze sind für **körperbehinderte** Menschen.

2 New words and phrases
▶ SB, p. 50 | VOCABULARY pp. 229–230

1	I want to buy the new book _____ my favourite author.	Ich möchte das neue Buch **von** meiner Lieblingsautorin kaufen.
2	I don't like the _____ of the room.	Ich mag den **Stil** des Raumes nicht.
3	Tim doesn't wear _____ jackets.	Tim trägt keine **engen** Jacken.
4	Sean _____ dogs _____ cats.	Sean **hat** Hunde **lieber als** Katzen.
5	My dad's blazer is too _____ on me.	Der Blazer meines Vaters ist mir zu **weit**.
6	You'll be warmer with _____!	Mit einer **Strumpfhose** wird dir wärmer sein.
7	The pink letters _____ well against the black T-shirt.	Die rosafarbenen Buchstaben **heben sich** gut vom schwarzen T-Shirt **ab**.
8	_____ colours look good on me.	**Helle** Farben stehen mir gut.
9	Would these trousers look good with a _____ shirt?	Würde diese Hose gut zu einem **gemusterten** Hemd aussehen?
10	Maya bought that _____ dress in a second-hand shop.	Maya hat dieses **altmodische** Kleid in einem Secondhandladen gekauft.
11	I like Tim's _____ style.	Ich mag Tims **schlichten** Stil.
12	Your new dress is very _____!	Dein neues Kleid ist sehr **attraktiv**!

▶ Check

3 School show

Complete the text for each picture. Use the words from the box.

> baggy • by • fashion • fashioned • light • patterned • plain •
> prefer • stand out from • style • tight • tights

Welcome to our school's _____ show!

Big, _____ shirts are very cool right now. You can just buy your shirts three sizes too large!

_____ under shorts are a great look.

_____ green sunglasses are a brave statement!

That old-_____ skirt looks like something my grandma wore!

And my grandpa wore _____ ties like that back in the 1970s!

Mike looks like his shoes are too _____!

The _____ brown blazer is a little boring, I think.

That boy in the blue shorts really _____ _____ the others!

We love this sporty _____!

Sheri _____ jeans to dresses.

We hope you've all enjoyed this fashion show _____ our students.

4 New words and phrases

▶ SB, pp. 51–52 | VOCABULARY pp. 230–231

1 Our English teacher is a big fan of

_____.

Unser Englischlehrer ist ein großer Fan von

Diktaten.

2 Denise only bought one new piece of

_____ last year.

Denise hat letztes Jahr nur ein neues

Kleidungsstück gekauft.

3 A small _____

of our clothes gets recycled.

Ein kleiner **Prozentsatz** unserer Kleidung wird

recycelt.

4 A shower uses 60 _____

of water in about five minutes.

Eine Dusche verbraucht 60 **Liter** Wasser in ungefähr

fünf Minuten.

5 I don't like the _____

of this shirt.

Mir gefällt der **Stoff** dieses Shirts nicht.

6 This _____ of the

story is really funny, but the rest isn't.

Dieser **Teil** der Geschichte ist wirklich lustig, der

Rest aber nicht.

7 _____ is

usually a lot cheaper than

_____.

Baumwolle ist normalerweise viel günstiger als

Seide.

8 Riley gave me a _____

answer.

Riley gab mir eine **schnelle** Antwort.

9 A lot of _____

_____ have closed

because people buy online.

Viele **Kaufhäuser** haben geschlossen, weil die Leute

online kaufen.

10 If you _____

that, you can sell it online.

Wenn du das **reparierst**, kannst du es online

verkaufen.

11 That's a good bag. You should

_____ it.

Das ist eine gute Tasche.

Du solltest sie **wiederverwenden**.

12 We _____

bottles into cute lamps.

Wir **upcyceln** Flaschen zu

süßen Lampen.

13 This _____ makes clothes

for _____ brands.

Diese **Fabrik** stellt Kleidung für **mehrere** Marken

her.

14 We _____ about five

hundred _____ hats a day.

Wir **produzieren** etwa fünfhundert **identische**

Mützen pro Tag.

15 Fred wants a _____

brand of jeans.

Fred möchte eine **bestimmte** Jeansmarke.

▶ Check ⤵

5 New words and phrases

▶ SB, p. 53 | VOCABULARY pp. 231–232

1 This bridge was built _____

_____.

Diese Brücke wurde **im 18. Jahrhundert** errichtet.

2 Old _____

were loud and dangerous.

Alte **Baumwollfabriken** waren laut und gefährlich.

3 Frannie wants to be a

_____ designer.

Frannie möchte **Textil**designerin werden.

4 This story doesn't make any

_____.

Diese Geschichte ergibt keinen **Sinn**.

5 Dan works in the fashion

_____.

Dan arbeitet in der Mode**industrie**.

6 The sun was already _____

in the sky at 5 p.m.

Die Sonne stand um 17 Uhr bereits **tief** am

Himmel.

7 How high is the _____

here? The _____ is

great!

Wie hoch ist die **Miete** hier? Der **Ort** ist toll!

8 I ate the sandwich _____

I didn't like it.

Ich habe das Sandwich gegessen, **obwohl** ich es

nicht mochte.

9 Our library organized a book

_____ to earn money.

Unsere Bibliothek organisierte einen

Bücher**verkauf**, um Geld einzunehmen.

10 These shoes are expensive and,

_____,

they're not comfortable.

Diese Schuhe sind teuer und **außerdem** sind sie

nicht bequem.

11 Several _____ singers

live here.

Hier leben mehrere **bekannte** Sänger und

Sängerinnen.

12 An _____ of airplanes

is that they're fast, but a

_____ is

that they pollute the air.

Ein **Vorteil** von Flugzeugen ist,

dass sie schnell sind, aber ein

Nachteil ist, dass sie die Luft

verschmutzen.

13 Our supermarket has some great

_____ this week.

Unser Supermarkt hat diese Woche einige

tolle **Angebote**.

14 Fast fashion is bad for the

_____.

Fast Fashion ist schlecht für die **Umwelt**.

6 New words and phrases

▶ SB, p. 54 | VOCABULARY pp. 232–233

1 _____ is the best gift.

Freundschaft ist das beste Geschenk.

2 Mason always _____ good _____ .

Mason **gibt** immer gute **Ratschläge**.

3 You _____ help me cook. I enjoy it!

Du **brauchst** mir **nicht** beim Kochen zu helfen. Es macht mir Spaß!

4 Read this book. It _____ help you understand the topic better.

Lies dieses Buch. Es **könnte** dir helfen, das Thema besser zu verstehen.

5 _____ are always happy about presents.

Man freut sich immer über Geschenke.

6 _____ should always have an umbrella with you.

Man sollte immer einen Regenschirm dabei haben.

7 _____ say it's going to snow.

Man sagt, dass es schneien wird.

8 I don't have any real _____ , but I have some _____ .

Ich habe keine echten **Feinde**, aber ich habe einige **falsche Freunde**.

9 Archie_____ Kiki, but Kiki isn't interested.

Archie **ist in** Kiki **verliebt**, aber Kiki hat kein Interesse.

10 _____ are always friendly but I don't know _____ name.

Er/Sie ist immer freundlich, aber ich kenne **seinen/ihren** Namen nicht.

11 Alex doesn't _____ as a boy or a girl.

Alex **identifiziert sich** weder als Junge noch als Mädchen.

7 Scrambled words

The letters in the blue words are mixed up. Put them in the right order and write them down. They all start with _p_.

1 Do you have any lanpi yoghurt? _____

2 A small racetnegep of people have red hair. _____

3 Her skirt is tpertaned with little dogs. _____

4 We ecduorp too much rubbish each year. _____

5 I reepfr chocolate to vanilla. _____

8 New words and phrases

▶ SB, pp. 55–57 | VOCABULARY pp. 233–234

1 Oskar _____ but I like him.　　Oskar **ist ein Nerd**, aber ich mag ihn.

2 Sam _____ but I am still angry.　　Sam **hat sich bei mir entschuldigt**, aber ich bin immer noch wütend.

3 Federico _____ you.　　Federico **vertraut** dir.

4 My parents aren't very _____.　　Meine Eltern sind nicht sehr **streng**.

5 I _____ in our neighbour's pool.　　Ich **darf** im Pool unseres Nachbarn **schwimmen**.

6 _____ my neighbour.　　**Ich bin in** meinen Nachbarn **verliebt**.

7 You _____ not like it, but I'm going to give you my opinion.　　Es gefällt dir **vielleicht** nicht, aber ich werde dir meine Meinung sagen.

8 Annie always _____ my jokes.　　Annie **versteht** meine Witze immer.

9 Can you _____ a banana for your little brother?　　Kannst du für deinen kleinen Bruder eine Banane **klein schneiden**?

10 Will they hear us if we _____?　　Werden sie uns hören, wenn wir **schreien**?

9 Running to the shop

Underline the right modal verb in each sentence.

1 I **might / should / can't** run to the shop, but I don't want to.

2 I **must / shouldn't / 'm allowed to** run to the shop: We need some milk fast!

3 I **'m allowed to / needn't / 'm not allowed to** run to the shop: It's too dangerous.

4 I **can't / might / must** run to the shop: I haven't decided yet.

5 I **needn't / 'm allowed to / can't** run to the shop: My foot hurts.

6 I **must / needn't / should** run to the shop: My brother already went.

7 I **'m not allowed to / can / 'm allowed to** run to the shop: I'm old enough.

8 I want to but I **shouldn't / should / must** run to the shop: It's better to walk.

10 New words and phrases

▶ SB, pp. 58–61 | VOCABULARY pp. 234–236

1 Talk directly into the _____.

Sprechen Sie direkt in das **Mikrofon**.

2 You can _____ the TV _____ now, but _____ it _____ again in half an hour.

Du kannst den Fernseher jetzt **einschalten**, aber **schalte** ihn in einer halben Stunde wieder **aus**.

3 My grandma has always been a _____ for me.

Meine Oma ist für mich immer ein **Vorbild** gewesen.

4 Megan is _____ the cleverest girl in our class.

Megan ist **sicherlich** das klügste Mädchen in unserer Klasse.

5 Can you _____ _____ for a few hours?

Kannst du **dich** für ein paar Stunden **beschäftigen**?

6 I've _____ all the money that I got for my birthday.

Ich habe das gesamte Geld **behalten**, das ich zu meinem Geburtstag bekommen habe.

7 Kai can't _____ anything secret.

Kai kann nichts geheim **halten**.

8 Finn_____! He should stop now!

Finn **singt dauernd**! Er soll jetzt damit aufhören!

9 Sophie _____ the _____ and our team lost the game.

Sophie **verschoss** den **Elfmeter** und unsere Mannschaft verlor das Spiel.

10 The weather is really _____ today. Let's stay home!

Das Wetter ist heute wirklich **scheußlich**. Lass uns zu Hause bleiben!

11 Come tomorrow or _____ you want.

Komm morgen oder **wann immer** du willst.

12 Our organization has helped hundreds of people out of _____.

Unsere Organisation hat Hunderten von Menschen aus der **Armut** geholfen.

13 My dogs always _____ when I open the door to the kitchen.

Meine Hunde **tauchen** immer **auf**, wenn ich die Tür zur Küche öffne.

14 The kids _____ in their seats now: They're very bored.

Die Kinder **lümmeln** jetzt auf ihren Plätzen. Sie langweilen sich sehr.

15 Lexi got a lot of nice _____ about her new skirt.

Lexi hat viele nette **Komplimente** für ihren neuen Rock bekommen.

11 Reflexive pronouns

Complete the text with the right reflexive pronouns and *each other*.

Make your own podcast: Find confidence in 1 _____

A podcast is a fun way to share ideas with the world. We have some tips

from successful podcasters Sarah Simon and Mark Jaxson for you and your

podcast journey.

It's normal to feel a bit nervous! Sarah's family and friends loved the

podcasts that she made for them, but it took Sarah a long time to believe

in 2 _____ and make a public one with Mark.

You might want to get a podcaster partner. If you do a podcast with a friend,

you can help 3 _____ to feel more confident.

"Find your voice!" says Mark. "I always tell 4 _____ to be Mark, not someone else!"

Talk about your interests and share your stories. Mark says that he understands 5 _____

better because of the podcast. Don't forget that a podcast should be fun. "Our listeners hear that we are

enjoying 6 _____ ... so they enjoy 7 _____ too!"

12 Definitions

Tick the right word for each definition.

1	a part or piece	bit	☐	plain	☐	offer	☐
2	not cool	low	☐	nerdy	☐	tight	☐
3	to believe that someone is honest	to trust	☐	to love	☐	to care	☐
4	to use a very loud voice	to talk	☐	to sigh	☐	to shout	☐
5	having a lot of rules	kind	☐	friendly	☐	strict	☐
6	everything around you, for example air, water, land, etc.	environment	☐	location	☐	sense	☐
7	You use this to make clothes.	jeans	☐	wardrobe	☐	material	☐
8	You pay this to live in a house or use a building.	price	☐	rent	☐	sale	☐
9	You really don't like this person.	enemy	☐	friend	☐	crush	☐

13 Opposites

Write the opposite words.

1 switch on ◄► _____

2 friend ◄► _____

3 modern ◄► _____

4 tight ◄► _____

5 (to) break ◄► _____

6 slow ◄► _____

14 New words and phrases

► SB, p. 62 | VOCABULARY p. 236

1 I've never had a _____ with my best friend.

Ich hatte noch nie einen **Streit** mit meiner besten Freundin.

2 You want me to wear pink? _____!

Du willst, dass ich Rosa trage? **Auf keinen Fall!**

3 _____! We'll be late!

Na los! Wir werden zu spät kommen!

4 Andrew stopped to _____ himself in the mirror.

Andrew blieb stehen, um sich im Spiegel zu **bewundern**.

5 There was a long _____ at the supermarket today.

Heute gab es eine lange **Schlange** im Supermarkt.

🔊 15 Listen carefully!
04

Listen carefully to the sentences and write the right word in each gap.

1 Are you _____ to take that?

2 That shirt is too _____ for me: I prefer a much different _____!

3 We stood in the _____ for an hour before the game.

4 My _____ is to stand up straight: Don't _____!

5 What _____ of kids in our class like to play video games?

It's _____ high!

6 After a short _____, the birds shared the worm.

7 I missed the _____ for our team.

8 We play in a basketball team for kids with _____.

9 You can _____ old clothes into so many cool things! You can also _____ them and keep wearing them!

► Check

16 Rhyming words

Underline the word that doesn't rhyme with the other three words in each line. Then find a word in the box that rhymes with the other three words.

buy • detail • do • go • may • quite • wheelchair

1   queue – flew – know – to

2   tight – eight – write – light

3   by – bye – sigh – sea

4   repair – nowhere – appear – software

5   throw – now – grow – oh

6   they – grey – try – day

7   sale – email – rail – sell

17 The right word

Underline the right word for each sentence.

1   Can you **hold / keep / make** a secret?

2   You can visit me **whenever / whoever / whatever** you want.

3   We stood in the **clue / queue / cloud** for a long time.

4   Nicki is **certainly / quickly / strictly** good at football.

5   The other team missed the **poverty / penalty / industry**.

6   Milo was very **nasty / nerdy / baggy** to his enemies.

7   What's the reason for the **cotton / pattern / conflict**?

8   I love to give **trust / compliments / sense** to make people feel good.

9   Millions of people around the world live in **poverty / industry / factories**.

10 I **identify / shout / admire** Jim's work a lot.

11 A strange message **appeared / slouched / repaired** on my phone today.

18 Almost the same

Match the sentences that have similar meanings.

1   That outfit is very attractive.

2   All of the houses in my street are identical.

3   This is a great location.

4   I want to give you some advice.

5   Don't slouch in your chair!

a   This is a wonderful place.

b   I would like to offer you some suggestions.

c   Please sit up.

d   Those clothes look very good together.

e   The buildings where I live are all the same.

19 New words and phrases

▶ SB, pp. 63–64 | VOCABULARY pp. 236–237

1 Another team is using the _____.

Eine andere Mannschaft benutzt das **Spielfeld**.

2 Our team was three points behind at _____.

Unser Team lag zur **Halbzeit** drei Punkte zurück.

3 I read whenever I get the _____. I love books!

Ich lese, wann immer ich die **Gelegenheit** habe. Ich liebe Bücher!

4 Cara is a great _____. No balls get in the _____!

Cara ist eine tolle **Torhüterin**. Kein Ball kommt ins **Netz**!

5 The fans _____ loudly for every goal.

Die Fans **jubelten** lautstark über jedes Tor.

6 Check the website if you need _____ information.

Schau dir die Webseite an, wenn du **zusätzliche** Informationen brauchst.

7 _____ that our team wins today!

Drück die Daumen, dass unser Team heute gewinnt!

8 Everyone _____ after the prime minister's speech.

Alle **klatschten** nach der Rede des Premierministers.

9 It's not nice to _____ _____.

Es ist nicht nett, **jemanden zu beschimpfen**.

10 My parents always _____ me _____ shout.

Meine Eltern **sagen** mir immer, **dass ich nicht** schreien **soll**.

11 Keep your _____ opinions to yourself!

Behaltet eure **rassistischen** Meinungen für euch!

12 You have to _____ on that door!

Du musst an der Tür **ziehen**!

13 Toby ran _____ to the kitchen after school.

Toby rannte nach der Schule **direkt** in die Küche.

14 I can _____ one cat, but not with six!

Ich **komme mit** einer Katze **klar**, aber nicht mit sechs!

15 Don't _____ the other students.

Unterbrich die anderen Schüler/innen nicht.

16 I don't like my _____ in this photo.

Mir gefällt meine **Pose** auf diesem Foto nicht.

▶ Check

20 Match the word parts

Match the parts to make longer words. Then write the words. Careful: Some words have a space between the parts and some have a hyphen (-)!

1	old	known	*old-fashioned*
2	department	keeper	_____
3	well	model	_____
4	role	fashioned	_____
5	class	cycle	_____
6	half	mate	_____
7	goal	store	_____
8	up	time	_____

21 Lost words

Complete the sentences with the right prepositions from the box.

> off • on (2x) • out • to (2x) • up • with (2x)

1 Georgia has a crush _____ James.

2 She prefers him _____ Larry.

3 She's not in love _____ James, though.

4 Georgia said sorry _____ Larry after she cut _____ his love letter. That wasn't nice!

5 Larry wanted to stand _____ with his letter.

6 Georgia tried to call James, but James switched _____ his phone. He didn't want to deal _____ the situation.

7 "Come _____," Georgia thought. "Answer your phone!"

22 Find the mistakes

There are two MISTAKES in each sentence. Underline and correct them.

1 Ethan upcykles old clothing into new fashuns. _____ _____

2 The waiter delt with severil problems. _____ _____

3 Please don't interupt: Jacob has the mikrophone. _____ _____

4 The fans cheared when the other team missed the penelty. _____ _____

23 New words and phrases

▶ SB, pp. 65–66 | VOCABULARY p. 238

1 We took a _____ from Manchester to London.

Wir sind mit einem **Reisebus** von Manchester nach London gefahren.

2 They stopped at a _____ _____ on the way to Brighton.

Sie hielten auf dem Weg nach Brighton an einer **Tankstelle**.

3 My mum always has an extra _____ in her car.

Meine Mutter hat immer einen Ersatz**reifen** in ihrem Auto.

4 I love a little _____ in savoury dishes!

Ich liebe ein bisschen **Ananas** in herzhaften Gerichten!

5 I _____ understand the problem, but I can't help you.

Ich verstehe das Problem **völlig**, aber ich kann dir nicht helfen.

6 _____ each sentence with a word from the list.

Vervollständige jeden Satz mit einem Wort aus der Liste.

7 Is our group _____?

Ist unsere Gruppe **vollständig**?

8 Fred _____ some good _____.

Fred **brachte** einige gute **Argumente vor**.

24 New words and phrases

▶ SB, p. 67 | VOCABULARY pp. 238–239

1 Noel _____ pizza, but I wanted pasta.

Noel **sprach sich für** Pizza **aus**, aber ich wollte Pasta.

2 Tom _____ his hair himself yesterday. It looks great!

Tom **hat** sich gestern die Haare selbst **geschnitten**. Das sieht toll aus!

3 I _____ the problem quickly yesterday.

Ich **bin** gestern **mit** dem Problem schnell **fertiggeworden**.

4 The kids _____ on their way home from school.

Die Kinder **froren** auf dem Heimweg.

5 I _____ his face but not his name.

Ich **kannte** sein Gesicht, aber nicht seinen Namen.

▶ Check ⬐

25 Irregular verbs

Write the past participle (third form) of each verb in the grid. Then put the letters from the blue boxes in the right order to find the solution.

1 become • 2 throw • 3 speak •
4 write • 5 freeze • 6 fall •
7 keep • 8 cut

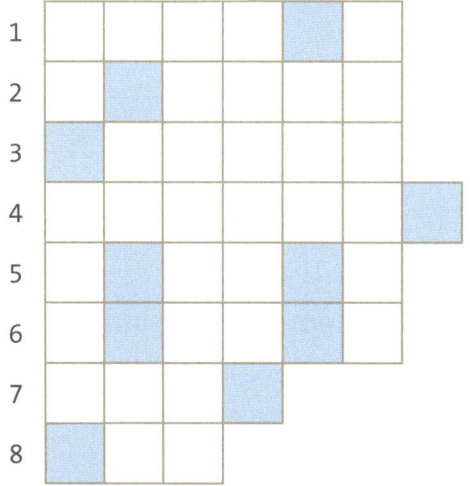

Solution: _____ is a city in England.

26 At a football game ↓ ← → ↘

What things and actions can you see at a football game? Find and write seven words.

N	X	M	P	E	N	A	L	T	Y
E	C	Z	S	R	H	C	T	I	P
T	Z	H	D	U	C	B	B	Q	S
R	E	P	E	E	K	L	A	O	G
Q	U	E	U	E	Z	X	A	K	K
A	C	D	E	B	R	M	P	P	D

_____

_____

_____

_____

_____

_____

_____

27 Writing a description

Write a paragraph about this sweatshirt.
Use all of the words from the box!

baggy • blue • brand • car • clothing • cool • cotton • material •
nerdy • patterned • pink • silk • style • sweatshirt • warm • yellow

28 Let's talk: Seine Meinung äußern und diskutieren

▶ p. 212

Was sagst du auf Englisch, wenn du ...

1   ... jemandem recht geben möchtest? _____

2   ... eine Sache etwas anders siehst? _____

3   ... kurz mal nachdenken möchtest? _____

4   ... jemandem ganz und gar nicht zustimmst? _____

5   ... ein Argument gut findest? _____

29 Let's talk: Über Interessen und Dinge sprechen, die einem wichtig sind
Über Probleme sprechen und Ratschläge erteilen

▶ p. 207 and p. 210

Maddie needs some advice. Complete the dialogue with phrases from the box.

I understand that. • You're welcome! • The problem is that ... • Could you help me, please? •
What's the most important thing to you? •
I think that's good advice. • You should ... • ... is really important to me because ...

I'm so stressed! 1 _____
_____ I need
some advice!

Of course! What's the problem?

2 _____ I never
have enough time for my homework.

Why not?

I do a lot of sport. And I like to relax and
look at my phone, see what my friends are
doing.

3 _____
4 _____
_____

Sport 5 _____
_____
it makes me feel good!

6 _____ make a
timetable. Write down specific times for
sport and homework. Then you'll see how
much time you have for your phone and
friends.

7 _____
_____
I'll try it. Thank you!

8 _____

▶ Check

ADVANCED

lighthouse 3

Wordmaster

Lösungen

Cornelsen

Hello! Where we're from

1 New words and phrases ▶ pp. 10–11 | VOCABULARY p. 218
1 south • 2 east; west • 3 Northern • 4 Republic • 5 Gaelic • 6 official

2 Directions
1 north • 2 west • 3 north • 4 west • 5 east • 6 south-west • 7 south-east • 8 south

3 New words and phrases ▶ pp. 12–13 | VOCABULARY pp. 218–219
1 bagpipes • 2 lake • 3 skyscraper • 4 mural • 5 boat • 6 canal • 7 foreground; background •
8 European Union • 9 vote; close • 10 exit • 11 regional • 12 remain/stay

4 Odd word out
1 talk • 2 swim • 3 skyscraper • 4 story • 5 boat • 6 underground

5 Listen carefully!
1 northern • 2 Gaelic • 3 exit • 4 republic • 5 official • 6 mural • 7 canal • 8 foreground • 9 close •
10 close

6 Definitions
1 close • 2 mural • 3 remain • 4 regional • 5 republic • 6 vote • **Solution:** Europe

Unit 1 London: City life

1 New words and phrases ▶ SB, pp. 14–15 | VOCABULARY pp. 219–220
1 acrobats • 2 parliament • 3 sculpture • 4 slide; slide • 5 tunnel • 6 ride • 7 wheels • 8 bank •
9 stall

2 Silhouettes
1 sculpture • 2 wheel • 3 tunnel • 4 slide • 5 acrobat • 6 stall

3 New words and phrases ▶ SB, p. 16 | VOCABULARY pp. 220–221
1 because of • 2 traffic; decided • 3 Travelcard • 4 escalators • 5 tube • 6 Wi-Fi • 7 Mind • 8 gap •
9 public • 10 local • 11 tram

4 New words and phrases ▶ SB, pp. 17–18 | VOCABULARY p. 221
1 Let • 2 lift • 3 lift • 4 direct • 5 indirect • 6 line • 7 ladies and gentlemen • 8 Throw

5 New words and phrases ▶ SB, p. 19 | VOCABULARY pp. 221–222
1 about • 2 billions • 3 millions; who • 4 almost • 5 system • 6 rail service • 7 double •
8 double-decker (bus) • 9 double room • 10 luggage • 11 cab/taxi • 12 take a test • 13 hire •
14 cross • 15 cross

6 The right verb
1 take a test • 2 throw • 3 cross • 4 decide • 5 let • 6 slide • 7 lift

7 Definitions
1 about • 2 lift • 3 system • 4 million • 5 (to) mind • 6 luggage • 7 billion • 8 rail

8 New words and phrases

▶ SB, p. 20 | VOCABULARY pp. 222–223

1 form • **2** includes • **3** including • **4** sites/places • **5** golden • **6** young • **7** prince • **8** royal • **9** King • **10** queen • **11** princess • **12** classic • **13** prime minister • **14** except (for) • **15** possible

9 Lost letters

1 Because • **2** traffic • **3** tube • **4** direct • **5** line • **6** Travelcard • **7** lift • **8** luggage • **9** escalator

10 New words and phrases

▶ SB, p. 21 | VOCABULARY p. 223

1 Push • **2** push • **3** handle • **4** conditions

11 That's what will happen!

1 parliament • **2** prime minister • **3** hire • **4** site • **5** mind • **6** push • **7** local • **8** billion • **9** gap

12 New words and phrases

▶ SB, p. 22 | VOCABULARY p. 223

1 tip; tips • **2** Saint/St • **3** central • **4** pelican • **5** fresh

13 New words and phrases

▶ SB, p. 23 | VOCABULARY pp. 223–224

1 virtual • **2** road • **3** roundabout • **4** column • **6** guards; guard • **6** capsule • **7** along the road

14 New words and phrases

▶ SB, pp. 24–25 | VOCABULARY pp. 224–225

1 homeless • **2** peaceful; colourful • **3** without • **4** care • **5** cares • **6** goal • **7** sustainable • **8** community • **9** less • **10** few • **11** little • **12** bike lanes • **13** air pollution • **14** lead • **15** make; the leader

15 Listen carefully!

1 columns • **2** site • **3** except • **4** decide • **5** escalator • **6** double • **7** guard • **8** wheel • **9** pelicans; local • **10** sustainable

16 Groups of three

1 pollution • **2** homeless • **3** cab • **4** less • **5** air • **6** road

17 Rhyming words

1 bridge • **2** hear • **3** eight • **4** health

18 New words and phrases

▶ SB, pp. 26–27 | VOCABULARY p. 226

1 tap • **2** tap water; sparkling • **3** soft • **4** soft drinks • **5** mint • **6** plates • **7** aubergine(s) • **8** cucumber • **9** olives • **10** sesame • **11** I'll have • **12** ordered; waiter; waitress • **13** introduce • **14** introduction • **15** paragraph

19 New words and phrases

▶ SB, pp. 28–30 | VOCABULARY pp. 226–228

1 statues • **2** right after school • **3** doorkeeper • **4** shake • **5** shook • **6** towards • **7** natural • **8** grass • **9** sighed • **10** hurried • **11** route • **12** clues • **13** path • **14** bench • **15** similar

20 New words and phrases

▶ SB, p. 31 | VOCABULARY p. 228

1 volunteers • **2** volunteer • **3** recognize • **4** makes a difference

21 Categories

1 bench, grass, statue • **2** aubergine, cucumber, olive • **3** cab, tram, tube • **4** king, prince, queen

22 Word families

1 (to) mind • **2** air • **3** pollution • **4** sparkling • **5** introduction; (to) introduce • **6** opposite •
7 volunteer; (to) volunteer • **8** public

23 New words and phrases
▶ SB, pp. 32–33 | VOCABULARY pp. 228–229

1 searched • **2** recent • **3** recently • **4** government • **5** company • **6** wax; figures • **7** regular •
8 copy • **9** agency • **10** voice

24 Listen carefully!

1 sesame; plates • **2** statue; similar • **3** cucumbers • **4** paragraph; introduces • **5** wax; voices •
6 towards • **7** agency

25 Verb walk

decided • led • searched • sighed • included • copied • volunteered • shook • let • hired •
minded • lifted • made • slid • cared • rode

26 Opposites

1 similar / the same • **2** soft/easy • **3** impossible • **4** less • **5** few • **6** without • **7** direct • **8** young •
9 gentlemen • **10** recently

27 Giving directions

1 along • **2** turn • **3** straight • **4** past • **5** see • **6** right • **7** across • **8** left • **9** bridge • **10** left •
11 river

28 Let's talk: Essen gehen und in einem Restaurant bestellen
▶ SB, p. 209

(Lösungsbeispiel)
I'll have the spicy sausages with lemon, please. • Yes, I'm allergic to **milk. / No, I don't.** • I'll have the
salad, please. • Yes, **I'll have some sparkling water, please.** • **Thank you.**

Unit 2 Manchester: Who we are

1 New words and phrases
▶ SB, pp. 48–49 | VOCABULARY p. 229

1 fashion • **2** kindness • **3** disability • **4** disabled

2 New words and phrases
▶ SB, p. 50 | VOCABULARY pp. 229–230

1 by • **2** style • **3** tight • **4** prefers; to / likes; better than • **5** baggy • **6** tights • **7** stand out • **8** Light •
9 patterned • **10** old-fashioned • **11** plain • **12** attractive

3 School show

1 fashion • **2** baggy • **3** Tights • **4** Light • **5** (old-)fashioned • **6** patterned • **7** tight • **8** plain •
9 stands out from • **10** style • **11** prefers • **12** by

4 New words and phrases
▶ SB, pp. 51–52 | VOCABULARY pp. 230–231

1 dictations • **2** clothing • **3** percentage • **4** litres • **5** material • **6** bit/part • **7** cotton; silk • **8** quick •
9 department stores • **10** repair • **11** reuse • **12** upcycle • **13** factory; several • **14** produce; identical •
15 specific

5 New words and phrases
▶ SB, p. 53 | VOCABULARY pp. 231–232

1 in the 1700s • 2 cotton mills • 3 textile • 4 sense • 5 industry • 6 low • 7 rent; location • 8 (al)though • 9 sale • 10 in addition • 11 well-known • 12 advantage; disadvantage • 13 offers • 14 environment

6 New words and phrases
▶ SB, p. 54 | VOCABULARY pp. 232–233

1 Friendship • 2 gives; advice • 3 needn't • 4 might • 5 People • 6 You • 7 They/People • 8 enemies; frenemies • 9 is in love with • 10 They; their • 11 identify

7 Scrambled words

1 plain • 2 percentage • 3 patterned • 4 produce • 5 prefer

8 New words and phrases
▶ SB, pp. 55–57 | VOCABULARY pp. 233–234

1 is nerdy • 2 said sorry to me • 3 trusts • 4 strict • 5 'm allowed to swim • 6 I have a crush on / I'm in love with • 7 might • 8 gets • 9 cut up • 10 shout

9 Running to the shop

1 should • 2 must • 3 'm not allowed to • 4 might • 5 can't • 6 needn't • 7 'm allowed to • 8 shouldn't

10 New words and phrases
▶ SB, pp. 58–61 | VOCABULARY pp. 234–236

1 microphone • 2 switch; on; switch; off • 3 role model • 4 certainly • 5 keep yourself busy • 6 kept • 7 keep • 8 keeps singing • 9 missed; penalty • 10 nasty • 11 whenever • 12 poverty • 13 appear • 14 are slouching • 15 compliments

11 Reflexive pronouns

1 yourself • 2 herself • 3 each other • 4 myself • 5 himself • 6 ourselves • 7 themselves

12 Definitions

1 bit • 2 nerdy • 3 to trust • 4 to shout • 5 strict • 6 environment • 7 material • 8 rent • 9 enemy

13 Opposites

1 switch off • 2 enemy • 3 old-fashioned • 4 baggy • 5 (to) repair • 6 quick/fast

14 New words and phrases
▶ SB, p. 62 | VOCABULARY p. 236

1 conflict • 2 No way! • 3 Come on! • 4 admire • 5 queue

15 Listen carefully!

1 allowed • 2 plain; style • 3 queue • 4 advice; slouch • 5 percentage; certainly • 6 conflict • 7 penalty • 8 disabilities • 9 upcycle; repair

16 Rhyming words

1 know; do • 2 eight; quite • 3 sea; buy • 4 appear; wheelchair • 5 now; go • 6 try; may • 7 sell; detail

17 The right word

1 keep • 2 whenever • 3 queue • 4 certainly • 5 penalty • 6 nasty • 7 conflict • 8 compliments • 9 poverty • 10 admire • 11 appeared

18 Almost the same
1 d • 2 e • 3 a • 4 b • 5 c

19 New words and phrases
► SB, pp. 63–64 | VOCABULARY pp. 236–237

1 pitch • 2 half-time • 3 chance • 4 goalkeeper; net • 5 cheered • 6 additional • 7 Cross your fingers • 8 clapped (their hands) • 9 call someone/somebody names • 10 tell; not to • 11 racist • 12 pull • 13 straight/directly • 14 deal with • 15 interrupt • 16 pose

20 Match the word parts
1 old-fashioned • 2 department store • 3 well-known • 4 role model • 5 classmate • 6 half-time • 7 goalkeeper • 8 upcycle

21 Lost words
1 on • 2 to • 3 with • 4 to; up • 5 out • 6 off; with • 7 on

22 Find the mistakes
1 upcycles; fashions • 2 dealt; several • 3 interrupt; microphone • 4 cheered; penalty

23 New words and phrases
► SB, pp. 65–66 | VOCABULARY p. 238

1 coach • 2 service station • 3 tyre • 4 pineapple • 5 completely • 6 Complete • 7 complete • 8 made; points

24 New words and phrases
► SB, p. 67 | VOCABULARY pp. 238–239

1 argued for • 2 cut • 3 dealt with • 4 froze • 5 knew

25 Irregular verbs
1 become • 2 thrown • 3 spoken • 4 written • 5 frozen • 6 fallen • 7 kept • 8 cut
Solution: Manchester

26 At a football game

N	X	M	P	E	N	A	L	T	Y
E	C	Z	S	R	H	C	T	I	P
T	Z	H	D	U	C	B	B	Q	S
R	E	P	E	E	K	L	A	O	G
Q	U	E	U	E	Z	X	A	K	K
A	C	D	E	B	R	M	P	P	D

↓ net • → penalty • ← pitch • ↘ cheer • ↘ clap • ← goalkeeper/goal • → queue

27 Writing a description
(Lösungsbeispiel)
This is a **baggy blue sweatshirt**. It's **patterned** with **yellow, pink** and **blue cars**. It looks like a **warm** piece of **clothing** and the **material** is probably **cotton**, not **silk**. It's not really my **style**: It's a little **nerdy** and I like to look **cool**. You can't see the **brand**.

28 Let's talk: Seine Meinung äußern und diskutieren
► SB, p. 212

1 Yes, you're (so) right. / I think you're right. / I (completely) agree. • 2 I see it a bit differently. • 3 Just a minute. Let me think. • 4 I don't agree with you at all. / I completely disagree. • 5 That's a good point/argument.

29 Let's talk: Über Interessen und Dinge sprechen, die einem wichtig sind
Über Probleme sprechen und Ratschläge erteilen
Komplimente machen ▶ p. 207 and p. 210
(Lösungsbeispiel)
1 Could you help me, please? • **2** The problem is that • **3** I understand that. • **4** What's the most important thing to you? • **5** is really important to me because • **6** You should • **7** I think that's good advice. • **8** You're welcome!

Unit 3 Scotland: Adventure

1 New words and phrases
▶ SB, pp. 80–82 | VOCABULARY pp. 239–241
1 kayak • **2** coast • **3** took notes • **4** made; notes • **5** carry • **6** legend • **7** creatures; mermaids • **8** deep • **9** loving • **10** seems to be; unfortunately; definitely • **11** sonar; centimetres • **12** hunted; eels • **13** fake; submarines • **14** catfish; however; Therefore / That's why • **15** mystery

2 New words and phrases
▶ SB, pp. 83–85 | VOCABULARY p. 241
1 waste • **2** waste • **3** mediation • **4** translate • **5** translation • **6** communicate • **7** soldiers • **8** piper's

3 Word families
1 coast • **2** mystery • **3** deep • **4** loving/lovingly • **5** definitely • **6** (to) hunt • **7** communication; (to) communicate

4 New words and phrases
▶ SB, pp. 86–87 | VOCABULARY pp. 241–242
1 cliff • **2** ski • **3** Pack • **4** adventurous • **5** catch • **6** (has) caught • **7** tent • **8** twice

5 Water words

C	K	S	P	O	T	W	X	M
R	A	I	N	T	W	I	C	E
L	Y	T	Q	Z	C	T	L	R
A	A	B	F	R	O	C	C	M
P	K	R	D	I	A	H	D	A
I	P	S	G	V	S	E	F	I
P	A	E	F	E	T	H	A	D
E	C	A	E	R	G	G	K	H
R	K	I	J	L	A	K	E	K
S	U	B	M	A	R	I	N	E

↘ catfish/fish • ↓ kayak • → rain •
↓ mermaid • ↓ coast • ↓ river • ↓ sea •
↘ eel • → lake • → submarine

6 New words and phrases
▶ SB, pp. 88–89 | VOCABULARY pp. 242–243
1 Skydiving; risky; for • **2** outdoor activity • **3** motivation • **4** jungle • **5** live volcano • **6** cave • **7** Rhinos • **8** since • **9** take part in • **10** serious • **11** scanned; e.g. • **12** period of time • **13** primary school • **14** biography

7 Odd word out
1 cave • 2 soldier • 3 fake • 4 funny • 5 coast • 6 singing • 7 rhino • 8 tent

8 New words and phrases
▶ SB, pp. 90–91 | VOCABULARY pp. 243–244

1 Plants • 2 (have) planted • 3 landscape • 4 Wild • 5 deer; deer • 6 countryside • 7 blueberries •
8 heather • 9 Scots

9 Rhyming words
1 cost; most • 2 juice; rice • 3 well; deal • 4 want; aunt • 5 wear; year • 6 say; key

10 Listen carefully!
1 twice • 2 serious • 3 therefore • 4 Unfortunately • 5 deer; heather • 6 biography • 7 adventurous;
jungle • 8 Soldiers • 9 definitely • 10 rhinos

11 New words and phrases
▶ SB, p. 92 | VOCABULARY p. 244

1 state • 2 pretty • 3 bitter • 4 shiny • 5 sour • 6 ugly; unusual • 7 wet • 8 salty

12 Nature and outdoor activities ABC
adventurous • blueberry • cliff • deer • eel • fishing • globe • heather • insects • jungle • kayak •
landscape • mountain climbing • nature • outdoor activity • plant • rhino • ski • tent •
underwater cave • volcano • wild • zip wire

13 New words and phrases
▶ SB, p. 93 | VOCABULARY pp. 244–245

1 on the fringe • 2 performance • 3 perform • 4 The Olympics / The Olympic games • 5 World Cup •
6 last • 7 absolute(ly) • 8 attends; church

14 New words and phrases
▶ SB, p. 94 | VOCABULARY pp. 245–246

1 before • 2 before • 3 whole • 4 trainers • 5 mean to hurt • 6 halfway

15 Crossword puzzle
Across: 2 salty • 6 sonar • 7 since • 10 mystery • 11 carry • 14 however • 15 fringe • 17 piper •
18 trainer • 19 whole • 20 ugly
Down: 1 scan • 3 translate • 4 risky • 5 waste • 8 church • 9 seem • 11 cliff • 12 deep • 13 deer •
16 rhino • 17 pretty

16 New words and phrases
▶ SB, p. 95 | VOCABULARY pp. 246–247

1 narrow • 2 ridge • 3 valley • 4 cried • 5 eventually • 6 calm down • 7 walk on • 8 slip • 9 rock •
10 in order to • 11 rescue • 12 helicopter • 13 fault • 14 loose • 15 at last • 16 lowered •
17 paramedics • 18 rope

17 Opposites
1 unfortunately • 2 usual • 3 fake • 4 unpack • 5 serious • 6 countryside • 7 before • 8 valley •
9 (to) calm down • 10 (to) cry

18 Letter code
Take a look at this **fake** photo of the **countryside**. I found it on the internet! At first it **seemed** to be real.
However, the **landscape** in the picture is **definitely** strange. Look at the little hill on the left. It looks like a
volcano, but there's water coming out of it. Very **unusual**! And the water in that small lake looks very
deep. What other mistakes can you find?

19 New words and phrases
▶ SB, pp. 96–98 | VOCABULARY pp. 247–248
1 choice • 2 chose • 3 summary • 4 contrast • 5 result • 6 Make sure (that) • 7 British Isles • 8 stormy • 9 develop

20 New words and phrases
▶ SB, p. 99 | VOCABULARY p. 248
1 fishing • 2 lifeguard • 3 digital • 4 rewrote • 5 taught • 6 shone

21 Listen carefully!
1 before • 2 whole • 3 summary • 4 ridge • 5 valley • 6 fault • 7 loose • 8 choice • 9 caught

22 Let's talk: Einen Konflikt lösen und sich entschuldigen
▶ SB, p. 210
(Lösungsbeispiel)
1 It's very dangerous / It's not safe to play with a knife/knives. • 2 Why did you do that / play with a knife? • 3 I'm glad/happy you are OK / not hurt / safe. • 4 That's OK. • 5 Next time you should check your calendar. • 6 I'm sorry, it was a bad idea to write you a nasty message.

Unit 4 Wales: Digital life

1 New words and phrases
▶ SB, pp. 114–115 | VOCABULARY p. 249
1 cable car • 2 waterfall • 3 coal • 4 mining • 5 ship • 6 voice-over

2 New words and phrases
▶ SB, pp. 116–117 | VOCABULARY pp. 249–250
1 exchange • 2 ours • 3 edit • 4 roller coaster • 5 theme • 6 actually • 7 melody • 8 rhythm • 9 detective

3 Possessive pronouns
1 ours • 2 His • 3 yours • 4 mine • 5 Hers • 6 yours; theirs

4 Scrambled words
1 actually • 2 theme • 3 exchange • 4 edit • 5 voice-over • 6 hers • **Solution:** detectives

5 New words and phrases
▶ SB, p. 119 | VOCABULARY pp. 250–251
1 watersport(s) • 2 excellent • 3 spot • 4 paddleboarding • 5 lovely/beautiful • 6 sand • 7 triathlon • 8 tens of thousands of people • 9 wave; rock pool • 10 edge • 11 explored

6 New words and phrases
▶ SB, pp. 120–121 | VOCABULARY p. 252
1 cardigan • 2 apron • 3 waistcoats • 4 gymnastics • 5 gymnast • 6 How are things

7 Crossword puzzle
1 cardigan • 2 gymnastics • 3 waterfall • 4 mining • 5 coal • 6 ship • 7 apron • 8 waistcoat

8 New words and phrases
▶ SB, p. 122 | VOCABULARY pp. 252–253
1 caption • 2 installed; installation • 3 charge; charger • 4 press • 5 swipe • 6 tap • 7 devices • 8 key • 9 document / (text) file

9 Categories
1 rock pool, sand, wave • 2 device, installation, key • 3 apron, cardigan, waistcoat • 4 gymnastics, paddleboarding, triathlon

10 Instructions
1 document • **2** Charge • **3** device • **4** Install • **5** Tap • **6** press • **7** connect

11 Listen carefully!
1 Coal • **2** caption • **3** exchange • **4** theirs • **5** theme • **6** actually • **7** edge

12 Odd word out
1 voice • **2** article • **3** car • **4** biking • **5** they • **6** paper • **7** shoes • **8** cable car

13 New words and phrases ▶ SB, p. 123 | VOCABULARY pp. 253–254
1 exact; exactly • **2** watch • **3** set up • **4** agreed to • **5** agreed to meet • **6** agree with me • **7** agreed on • **8** terms/conditions • **8** pair; with • **10** print (out); printer • **11** (to) format • **12** format • **13** simple/easy

14 New words and phrases ▶ SB, p. 124 | VOCABULARY p. 254
1 debate/discuss • **2** debate • **3** versus/v/vs/against • **4** subscribe to; channel • **5** forward • **6** keep/stay in touch • **7** (has) got in touch • **8** lost touch • **9** comment about/on • **10** well-being • **11** diary

15 Verbs
1 debate • **2** subscribe • **3** edit • **4** install • **5** explore

16 New words and phrases ▶ SB, p. 125 | VOCABULARY pp. 254–255
1 whom • **2** informal • **3** instead of • **4** profile • **5** Shall I • **6** There you go. • **7** Would you like me to

17 Definitions
1 diary • **2** (to) agree • **3** roller coaster • **4** (to) edit

18 Word groups
1 mediate: language, translate • **2** screen: tap, swipe • **3** keep in touch: email, phone • **4** well-being: happy, healthy • **5** time: watch, clock

19 New words and phrases ▶ SB, pp. 126–127 | VOCABULARY pp. 255–256
1 cyberbullying • **2** which/that • **3** statistics • **4** One in five • **5** victim • **6** allows • **7** invents • **8** prison • **9** emotional • **10** network; type of / kind of

20 Homonyms
1a too • **1b** two • **2a** witch • **2b** which • **3a** theirs • **3b** there's • **4a** one • **4b** won

21 New words and phrases ▶ SB, pp. 128–130 | VOCABULARY pp. 256–257
1 skimmed the text • **2** lie to • **3** type in • **4** as well as • **5** latest • **6** Who cares? • **7** truth • **8** deleted • **9** breath • **10** jealous of • **11** the only person; whose • **12** for once • **13** tool • **14** lighting

22 Find the mistakes
1 cable • **2** thousands • **3** excellent • **4** lovely

23 New words and phrases ▶ SB, p. 131 | VOCABULARY p. 257
1 series • **2** sews • **3** skin • **4** headpiece

24 New words and phrases ▶ SB, p. 132 | VOCABULARY pp. 257–258
1 flowing • **2** symbol • **3** abbreviations • **4** order • **5** habit • **6** stress • **7** (has) blocked • **8** sum up • **9** To begin with

25 New words and phrases
▶ SB, p. 133 | VOCABULARY p. 258
1 image; source • **2** began/started • **3** keep • **4** lay • **5** 've/have sewn

26 The fourth word
1 gymnastics • **2** (the) truth • **3** breath • **4** ours • **5** theirs • **6** (to) sew • **7** (to) look at

27 Listen carefully!
1 victim • **2** Cyberbullying • **3** abbreviations • **4** jealous • **5** lain • **6** Whose

28 Let's talk: Hilfe anbieten, erbitten und annehmen – ein Telefongespräch führen
▶ SB, p. 211 and p. 212
(Lösungsbeispiel)
1 Hi, Peter. How are things (with you)? / How are you? • **2** I can help you if you like. • **3** Yes. / No problem. Would you like me to show you how to make some accounts / do that on your phone? • **4** Are you free later? / Do you have time later? • **5** I can't hear you. The connection is bad. • **6** Yes. See you later.

Unit 5 Two Irelands: Together

1 New words and phrases
▶ SB, pp. 148–149 | VOCABULARY pp. 258–259
1 Catholic; Protestant • **2** rule • **3** The Troubles; checkpoints • **4** bed and breakfast / B&B • **5** recommend

2 New words and phrases
▶ SB, p. 150 | VOCABULARY pp. 259–260
1 abroad; passport • **2** identity card / ID card • **3** age • **4** advanced • **5** accommodation • **6** kettle • **7** belongs to

3 New words and phrases
▶ SB, p. 151 | VOCABULARY p. 260
1 (two) twin beds • **2** cooked breakfast • **3** guests • **4** buffet; cereals; cold meat • **5** form

4 New words and phrases
▶ SB, p. 152 | VOCABULARY pp. 260–261
1 deals with • **2** such as • **3** artwork(s) • **4** take down • **5** divide up; attraction

5 How do you spell it?
1 A recommend • **2 B** accommodation • **3 A** buffet • **4 C** kettle • **5 A** cereals • **6 C** dealt • **7 B** cold meat • **8 B** breakfast • **9 C** guest

6 A review of The Beyond B&B
1 bed and breakfast • **2** recommend • **3** twin beds • **4** kettle • **5** cooked breakfast • **6** guests • **7** buffet • **8** cereals • **9** cold meats • **10** bath

7 Travel ABC
abroad • **b**ed and breakfast • **c**heckpoint • **f**orm • **g**uest • **i**dentity card • **k**ettle • **p**assport • **r**ecommend • **t**win beds • Bre**x**it

8 Odd word out
1 Irish • **2** science • **3** name • **4** checkpoint • **5** pizza • **6** bed • **7** form • **8** rucksack

9 Almost the same
1 d • 2 a • 3 e • 4 b • 5 c

10 New words and phrases ▶ SB, pp. 154–157 | VOCABULARY pp. 261–262
1 aim/goal • 2 (dance) routine • 3 didn't; either • 4 Good luck; do well • 5 beat • 6 nervous •
7 flash • 8 confused • 9 Judges • 10 on purpose • 11 justice • 12 times • 13 spectacular

11 Definitions
1 to belong to • 2 to divide up • 3 advanced • 4 flash • 5 justice • 6 judge • 7 to beat

12 Listen carefully!
1 Troubles • 2 recommended • 3 justice • 4 accommodations • 5 guests • 6 buffet • 7 cereals •
8 aim • 9 confused • 10 age

13 New words and phrases ▶ SB, p. 158 | VOCABULARY p. 262
1 generate • 2 bright • 3 wooden • 4 rug • 5 cosy/comfortable • 6 curtains • 7 analyse

14 New words and phrases ▶ SB, p. 159 | VOCABULARY p. 263
1 advertisement/ad/advert • 2 features • 3 grammar • 4 informative • 5 beat / 've/have beaten •
6 hung out • 7 kept • 8 've/have; seen

Unit 3
Scotland: Adventure

1 New words and phrases

SB, pp. 80–82 | VOCABULARY pp. 239–241

1	We hired a _____ for the trip.	Wir haben für den Ausflug ein **Kajak** gemietet.
2	We travelled to the _____.	Wir sind an die **Küste** gereist.
3	I _____ during the lesson but I can't read them!	Ich **habe mir** während des Unterrichts **Notizen gemacht**, aber ich kann sie nicht lesen!
4	Bryan _____ some _____ about his great idea.	Bryan **machte sich** einige **Notizen** zu seiner tollen Idee.
5	The boat can _____ ten people.	Das Boot kann zehn Personen **befördern**.
6	Rory told me an old _____.	Rory erzählte mir eine alte **Legende**.
7	I don't believe in _____ like _____.	Ich glaube nicht an **Wesen** wie **Meerjungfrauen**.
8	The sea is very _____ here.	Das Meer ist hier sehr **tief**.
9	Logan gave me a _____ look.	Logan schenkte mir einen **liebevollen** Blick.
10	The shop _____ closed, _____. But it will _____ be open tomorrow.	Der Laden **scheint** geschlossen **zu sein** – **leider**. Aber er hat morgen **auf jeden Fall** geöffnet.
11	Callum uses _____ equipment to find fish. He found one that was 70 _____ long!	Callum verwendet **Sonar**geräte, um Fische zu finden. Er hat einen gefunden, der 70 **Zentimeter** lang war!
12	Ava _____ for _____.	Ava **jagte** nach **Aalen**.
13	That photo is _____! There are no _____ in the lake.	Das Foto ist **gefälscht**. Es gibt keine **U-Boote** in dem See.
14	The _____ keep the water clean; _____, they're a bit boring. _____ they're not my favourite fish.	Die **Welse** halten das Wasser sauber; sie sind **allerdings** ein bisschen langweilig. **Daher** sind sie nicht meine Lieblingsfische.
15	Daniel solved the _____ quickly.	Daniel löste das **Rätsel** schnell.

2 New words and phrases

▶ SB, pp. 83–85 | VOCABULARY p. 241

1 That game is a _____ of money!

Das Spiel ist eine Geld**verschwendung**!

2 Don't _____ your time: This thing doesn't work.

Verschwenden Sie nicht Ihre Zeit: Das hier funktioniert nicht.

3 Nick's friendly _____ helped us to understand each other.

Nicks freundliche **Vermittlung** hat uns geholfen, uns gegenseitig zu verstehen.

4 Can you please _____ this sentence for me?

Kannst du bitte diesen Satz für mich **übersetzen**?

5 I don't think this _____ is very good.

Ich finde, diese **Übersetzung** ist nicht sehr gut.

6 My friends _____ with each other well.

Meine Freunde **kommunizieren** gut miteinander.

7 The _____ wear green uniforms.

Die **Soldaten** tragen grüne Uniformen.

8 The people danced to the _____'s music.

Die Leute tanzten zur Musik des **Dudelsackspielers**.

3 Word families

Write a word from the same word family in each gap.
Careful: Some of the words have the same form!

	noun	verb	adjective or adverb
1		(to) coast	coastal
2		(to) mystify	mysterious
3	depth	(to) deepen	
4	love	(to) love	
5	definition	(to) define	
6	hunter		hunted
7			communicative

▶ Check

4 New words and phrases

▶ SB, pp. 86–87 | VOCABULARY pp. 241–242

1   The hikers admired the ocean from the
    _____ .

Die Wanderinnen bewunderten das Meer von der **Klippe** aus.

2   Angus loves to _____
    in the winter.

Angus liebt es, im Winter **Ski zu fahren**.

3   _____ everything
    that you need.

Pack alles **ein**, was du brauchst.

4   You seem to be quite
    _____ .

Du scheinst ziemlich **abenteuerlustig** zu sein.

5   Try to _____ the ball.

Versuch mal, den Ball zu **fangen**.

6   Maxine _____
    two fish in the lake.

Maxine **hat** zwei Fische im See **gefangen**.

7   We slept in the _____
    at the campsite.

Wir schliefen im **Zelt** auf dem Campingplatz.

8   I've already brushed my teeth
    _____ today.

Ich habe heute meine Zähne schon **zweimal** geputzt.

5 Water words → ↓ ↘

Find ten water words (for example creatures that live in water, kinds of water, places with water ...) in the grid and write them down. Don't write other words you find!

C	K	S	P	O	T	W	X	M
R	A	I	N	T	W	I	C	E
L	Y	T	Q	Z	C	T	L	R
A	A	B	F	R	O	C	C	M
P	K	R	D	I	A	H	D	A
I	P	S	G	V	S	E	F	I
P	A	E	F	E	T	H	A	D
E	C	A	E	R	G	G	K	H
R	K	I	J	L	A	K	E	K
S	U	B	M	A	R	I	N	E

_____

_____

_____

_____

_____

_____

_____

_____

_____

_____

6 New words and phrases

▶ SB, pp. 88–89 | VOCABULARY pp. 242–243

1 _____ is a _____ sport. Mhairi has done it _____ two years.

Fallschirmspringen ist ein **riskanter** Sport. Mhairi macht es **seit** zwei Jahren.

2 What's your favourite _____ _____?

Was ist deine liebste **Outdoor-Aktivität**?

3 Hal doesn't have any _____.

Hal hat keine **Motivation**.

4 Our garden looks like a _____.

Unser Garten sieht aus wie ein **Dschungel**.

5 There's a _____ _____ on the island, so you aren't allowed to visit it.

Es gibt auf der Insel einen **aktiven Vulkan**, deshalb darf man sie nicht besuchen.

6 Do any animals live in the _____?

Leben in der **Höhle** irgendwelche Tiere?

7 _____ are not good pets!

Nashörner sind keine guten Haustiere!

8 The park has been open _____ eight o'clock.

Der Park ist **seit** acht Uhr geöffnet.

9 We want to _____ a tour of Edinburgh.

Wir wollen **an** einer Stadtrundfahrt durch Edinburgh **teilnehmen**.

10 Dana has a _____ topic to discuss.

Dana hat ein **ernstes** Thema zu besprechen.

11 Aurora _____ the article and found information about the accident, _____ the time and place.

Aurora **überflog** den Artikel und fand Informationen zum Unfall, **z. B.** zu Zeitpunkt und Ort.

12 Freya worked a lot in a short _____.

Freya hat in einem kurzen **Zeitraum** viel gearbeitet.

13 My little sister is still in _____ _____.

Meine kleine Schwester besucht noch die **Grundschule**.

14 I'm just reading a _____ of Taylor Swift.

Ich lese gerade eine **Biografie** von Taylor Swift.

▶ Check

7 Odd word out

Underline the word in each group that doesn't go with the other words.

1 to carry – to pack – bag – cave

2 mermaid – soldier – ghost – witch

3 true – fake – real – right

4 serious – sad – funny – angry

5 coast – volcano – mountain – hill

6 singing – kayaking – skiing – skydiving

7 rhino – hamster – cat – dog

8 kayak – submarine – boat – tent

8 New words and phrases

▶ SB, pp. 90–91 | VOCABULARY pp. 243–244

1 _____ make a room look nicer.

Pflanzen lassen einen Raum schöner aussehen.

2 We _____ tomatoes in our garden this year and they're really delicious.

Wir **haben** dieses Jahr im Garten Tomaten **gepflanzt** und sie sind wirklich lecker.

3 I love this _____ with its mountains and rivers.

Ich liebe diese **Landschaft** mit ihren Bergen und Flüssen.

4 _____ animals live in the mountains.

In den Bergen leben **wilde** Tiere.

5 We saw a _____ in the forest today. Yesterday we even saw two _____ !

Wir haben heute im Wald ein **Reh** gesehen. Gestern haben wir sogar zwei **Rehe** gesehen!

6 You can have a big garden in the _____ .

Auf dem **Land** kannst du einen großen Garten haben.

7 I sometimes put _____ in my yogurt.

Ich tue manchmal **Blaubeeren** in meinen Joghurt.

8 Is this purple plant _____ ?

Ist diese lila Pflanze **Heidekraut**?

9 People speak _____ and English here.

Die Leute sprechen hier **Schottisch** und Englisch.

9 Rhyming words

Underline the word that doesn't rhyme with the other three words in each line. Then find a word in the box that rhymes with the other three words.

| aunt • deal • key • |
| most • rice • year |

1   toast – coast – ghost – cost   _____

2   nice – price – juice – twice   _____

3   eel – feel – we'll – well   _____

4   plant – want – can't – chant   _____

5   pier – wear – deer – cheer   _____

6   say – ski – free – tea   _____

🔊 10 Listen carefully!
05

Listen carefully to the sentences and write the right word in each gap.

1   Esme ran around the park _____.

2   James had a _____ topic to talk about.

3   I'm ill and will _____ not come tonight.

4   _____, it rained on our picnic day.

5   A _____ jumped through the _____.

6   I read a _____ of Sir Arthur Conan Doyle, the author of the Sherlock

     Holmes stories.

7   My sister is very _____: She's visiting a _____

     now!

8   _____ fight for their country.

9   I will _____ do my chores after school.

10   We need to protect black _____.

▶ Check

11 New words and phrases

▶ SB, p. 92 | VOCABULARY p. 244

1 Our flat was in a bad _____ after the party.	Unsere Wohnung war nach der Feier in einem schlimmen **Zustand**.
2 Aren't those flowers _____?	Sind die Blumen nicht **hübsch**?
3 Grapefruit is too _____ for me.	Grapefruit ist mir zu **bitter**.
4 Tessa wore a pair of _____ black shoes.	Tessa trug **glänzende**, schwarze Schuhe.
5 I love the _____ taste of these lemons!	Ich liebe den **sauren** Geschmack dieser Zitronen!
6 In my opinion that is a very _____ sweatshirt. Maybe it's because of the _____ design.	Meiner Meinung nach ist das ein sehr **hässliches** Sweatshirt. Vielleicht liegt es an dem **ungewöhnlichen** Design.
7 We all got _____ in the rain.	Wir sind alle im Regen **nass** geworden.
8 Do you like _____ popcorn?	Magst du **salziges** Popcorn?

12 Nature and outdoor activities ABC

Complete the nature and outdoor activities ABC. You can find many of the words on pages 80–92.

13 New words and phrases

▶ SB, p. 93 | VOCABULARY pp. 244–245

1 The new shopping centre is _____ of the city.

Das neue Einkaufszentrum liegt **am Rande** der Stadt.

2 The _____ last night was great!

Die **Aufführung** gestern Abend war toll!

3 The actors _____ here every day.

Die Schauspieler **treten** hier jeden Tag **auf**.

4 _____ have never taken place in Scotland.

Die olympischen Spiele haben noch nie in Schottland stattgefunden.

5 We wanted to go to the _____ _____ but the tickets were too expensive.

Wir wollten zur **Weltmeisterschaft**, aber die Tickets waren zu teuer.

6 The party will _____ all weekend.

Die Feier wird das ganze Wochenende **dauern**.

7 I had the _____ worst day at school today!

Ich hatte heute den **absolut** schlimmsten Tag in der Schule.

8 Jane _____ _____ every Sunday.

Jane **geht** jeden Sonntag **zur Kirche**.

14 New words and phrases

▶ SB, p. 94 | VOCABULARY pp. 245–246

1 I think I've seen this film _____.

Ich glaube, dass ich diesen Film **schon einmal** gesehen habe.

2 Finish your homework _____ dinner.

Mach deine Hausaufgaben **vor** dem Abendessen fertig.

3 Our _____ school seems to be ill this week.

Unsere **ganze** Schule scheint diese Woche krank zu sein.

4 Cool _____! Are they comfortable?

Coole **Turnschuhe**! Sind sie bequem?

5 The dog didn't _____ _____ you. He just wanted to play.

Der Hund **hat** dich nicht **mit Absicht verletzt**. Er wollte nur spielen.

6 We are only _____ to our destination.

Wir sind erst **auf halbem Wege** zu unserem Ziel.

15 Crossword puzzle

Read the clues and write the words in the crossword.

Across:

2 Chips, crisps and seawater have this taste.

6 This thing uses sound to find sth. under water.

7 From a point in time until now.

10 You can't easily understand or explain one of these.

11 To have in your hand and bring with you, e.g. a bag.

14 Synonym of "but".

15 Far away from the centre = on the ???.

17 This person plays the bagpipes.

18 A shoe you wear for sports.

19 All (of sth.).

20 The opposite of beautiful.

Down:

1 To look for information in a text.

3 To change words from one language to another.

4 Synonym of "dangerous".

5 To not use (well), e.g. water, time, etc.

8 People pray in this building.

9 To look (like) or to appear to be.

11 The high, straight side of some hills or mountains, especially above water.

12 Very far down, especially in water.

13 This animal is shy and lives in the forest.

16 A large wild animal with one or two horns on its nose.

17 Synonym of "attractive".

16 New words and phrases

▶ SB, p. 95 | VOCABULARY pp. 246–247

1 The path through the forest is _____.

Der Weg durch den Wald ist **schmal**.

2 Euan and Lisa hiked to the top of the _____.

Euan und Lisa wanderten zur Spitze des **Bergkamms**.

3 There's no Wi-Fi in the _____.

Es gibt kein WLAN im **Tal**.

4 I _____ because I laughed so much.

Ich **weinte**, weil ich so sehr lachte.

5 If you keep practising, you'll _____ get better.

Wenn du weiter übst, wirst du **schließlich** besser.

6 It was hard to _____ after the scary film.

Es war schwer, **sich** nach dem Gruselfilm zu **beruhigen**.

7 Let's _____ and see the park.

Lass uns **weitergehen** und den Park anschauen.

8 Don't _____ on the wet floor.

Rutsch nicht auf dem nassen Boden **aus**.

9 We can't move that big _____.

Wir können den großen **Stein** nicht bewegen.

10 Felicia looked at the map _____ find the lake.

Felicia schaute sich die Karte an, **um** den See **zu** suchen.

11 The firefighters came with a _____ dog.

Die Feuerwehr kam mit einem **Rettungs**hund.

12 The _____ flew over the city.

Der **Hubschrauber** flog über die Stadt.

13 It's not your _____.

Es ist nicht deine **Schuld**.

14 These shoes feel too _____.

Diese Schuhe fühlen sich zu **locker** an.

15 They arrived _____ after a long journey.

Sie kamen **endlich** nach einer langen Reise an.

16 The firefighters carefully _____ Anna onto the ground.

Die Feuerwehrleute **ließen** Anna vorsichtig auf den Boden **hinunter**.

17 The _____ came quickly.

Die **Rettungssanitäter/innen** kamen schnell.

18 Both teams pulled on the _____.

Beide Teams zogen an dem **Seil**.

▶ Check

17 Opposites

Write the opposite words. Use only new words from this unit!

1 fortunately ◄ ► _____

2 unusual ◄ ► _____

3 real ◄ ► _____

4 pack ◄ ► _____

5 funny ◄ ► _____

6 city ◄ ► _____

7 after ◄ ► _____

8 mountain ◄ ► _____

9 (to) get excited ◄ ► _____

10 (to) laugh ◄ ► _____

18 Letter code

Every number matches a letter. Write the letters to complete the post.

Take a look at this <u>f</u> <u>a</u> <u>k</u> <u>e</u> photo of the
       1 2 3 4

<u>c</u> __ __ __ __ __ __ __ __ __.
5 6 7 8 9 10 11 12 13 14 4

I found it on the internet! At first it

<u>s</u> __ __ __ __ __ to be real.
12 4 4 15 4 14

<u>H</u> __ __ __ __ __, the
16 6 17 4 18 4 10

<u>l</u> __ __ __ __ __ __ __ __ in the
19 2 8 14 12 5 2 20 4

picture is <u>d</u> __ __ __ __ __ __ __ __ __ strange. Look at the little hill on the left. It looks
         14 4 1 13 8 13 9 4 19 11

like a __ __ __ __ __ __ __, but there's water coming out of it. Very __ __ __ __ __ __ __!
    18 6 19 5 2 8 6   7 8 7 12 7 2 19

And the water in that small lake looks very __ __ __ __. What other mistakes can you find?
                                   14 4 4 20

19 New words and phrases

▶ SB, pp. 96–98 | VOCABULARY pp. 247–248

1 My first _____ is always chocolate ice cream.

Meine erste **Wahl** ist immer Schokoladeneis.

2 Laurie _____ light colours for her room.

Laurie **wählte** helle Farben für ihr Zimmer.

3 Can you give me a short _____ of the book?

Kannst du mir eine kurze **Zusammenfassung** von dem Buch geben?

4 I like the _____ between the dark sky and the lights of the houses.

Ich mag den **Kontrast** zwischen dem dunklen Himmel und den Lichtern der Häuser.

5 Ellie hasn't seen the _____.

Ellie hat das **Ergebnis** nicht gesehen.

6 _____ the door is locked.

Stelle sicher, **dass** die Tür abgeschlossen ist.

7 About 72 million people live in the _____.

Ungefähr 72 Millionen Menschen leben auf den **Britischen Inseln**.

8 The weather was _____ all day.

Das Wetter war den ganzen Tag **stürmisch**.

9 Plants need sun to _____ well.

Pflanzen brauchen Sonne, um sich gut zu **entwickeln**.

20 New words and phrases

▶ SB, p. 99 | VOCABULARY p. 248

1 Ivan's hobby is _____.

Ivans Hobby ist **Angeln**.

2 Aisha has a summer job as a _____.

Aisha hat einen Sommerjob als **Rettungsschwimmerin**.

3 Modern cameras use _____ technology.

Moderne Kameras verwenden **digitale** Technologie.

4 I _____ the text last night to make it sound better.

Ich **habe** den Text gestern Abend **umgeschrieben**, damit er besser klingt.

5 Mrs Brown _____ English for twenty years.

Frau Brown **unterrichtete** zwanzig Jahre lang Englisch.

6 The sun _____ all day yesterday.

Die Sonne **schien** gestern den ganzen Tag.

▶ Check

21 Listen carefully!

Listen carefully to the sentences and write the right word in each gap.

1 We ate dinner _____ the film.

2 Phil read the _____ book in one night.

3 I didn't read the book, but I read a _____ of it.

4 The hikers reached the top of the _____.

5 The _____ doesn't get much sun.

6 The accident wasn't your _____.

7 These trousers are too _____.

8 I have to make a _____ between going to bed and staying up to play

video games.

9 Luke _____ the ball with one hand.

22 Let's talk: Einen Konflikt lösen und sich entschuldigen ▶ SB, p. 210

What can you say in these situations?

The situation	You say
1 Your brother played with a knife. You tell him that wasn't safe.	
2 You ask your brother why he played with a knife.	
3 You tell him you're happy that he's OK.	
4 Your friend said sorry for something that he did.	
5 Your friend forgot about your plans together. You suggest to your friend that she check her calendar in future situations.	
6 You wrote a nasty message to your friend and you know it was wrong.	

Unit 4
Wales: Digital life

1 New words and phrases

▶ SB, pp. 114–115 | VOCABULARY p. 249

1 We took the _____ | Wir fuhren mit der **Seilbahn** auf den Berg.
up the mountain.

2 Tourists love to visit the _____ | Touristen und Touristinnen besuchen gern den
because it's so beautiful. | **Wasserfall**, weil er so schön ist.

3 In the past, many people used | Früher nutzten viele Menschen **Kohle**, um ihre
_____ to make their homes warm. | Häuser zu beheizen.

4 There's no _____ in our town | Es gibt keinen **Bergbau** mehr in unserer Stadt.
anymore.

5 That _____ has a Welsh flag. | Das **Schiff** hat eine walisische Flagge.

6 The nature film has a German | Der Naturfilm hat eine deutsche **Off-Stimme**.
_____.

2 New words and phrases

▶ SB, pp. 116–117 | VOCABULARY pp. 249–250

1 I did an _____ to learn about | Ich habe einen **Austausch** gemacht, um etwas
a different culture. | über eine andere Kultur zu lernen.

2 Your class is big but _____ is small. | Eure Klasse ist groß, aber **unsere** ist klein.

3 I need to _____ my text. | Ich muss meinen Text **bearbeiten**.

4 I didn't feel very well after the _____ | Ich fühlte mich nicht sehr
_____. | wohl nach der **Achterbahn**.

5 The _____ of the film is love and | Das **Thema** des Films
friendship. | ist Liebe und Freundschaft.

6 No one believes me, but I _____ | Niemand glaubt es mir, aber **eigentlich** mag
like school! | ich die Schule!

7 That song has a beautiful _____. | Das Lied hat eine schöne **Melodie**.

8 Let's clap to the _____. | Lasst uns im **Rhythmus** klatschen.

9 The _____ found the | Die **Detektivin** hat das Geld gefunden.
money.

▶ Check

3 Possessive pronouns

Complete each sentence with the right possessive pronoun.

1 "This is my family's house:

   It's all _____."

2 "That's not Adam's jacket.

   _____ is blue."

3 "Is that laptop

   _____?"

4 "The red bicycle is

   _____."

5 Sophie loves dogs:

   _____ is the

   black one.

6 "Are these keys

   _____?"

   "No, they're _____."

4 Scrambled words

The letters in the blue words are mixed up. Put them in the right order and write them down. Then use the letters from the blue boxes to find the solution.

1 I cutlalay solved the puzzle very quickly.

2 The puzzle had a ehmet.

3 I had to acgenhex the places of the letters.

4 I then went back to tide some of my solutions.

5 It was like there was a ceoiv-revo helping me.

6 Anna did a puzzle too but resh was easier.

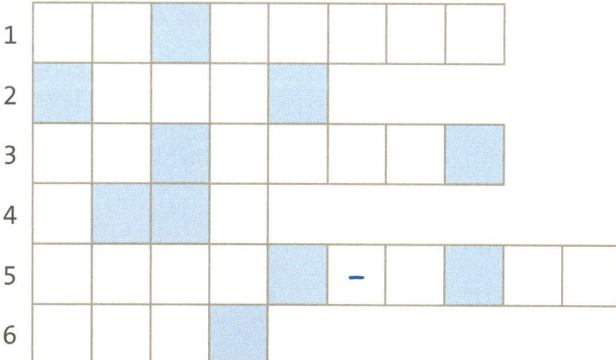

Solution: Only great word _____ can solve this puzzle!

5 New words and phrases

▶ SB, p. 119 | VOCABULARY pp. 250–251

1 Swimming, surfing and kayaking are all kinds of _____.

Schwimmen, Surfen und Kajakfahren sind alles Arten von **Wassersport**.

2 The beaches here are really

_____.

Die Strände hier sind wirklich **ausgezeichnet**.

3 My favourite _____ on this beach is on the northern end.

Meine Lieblings**stelle** an diesem Strand ist am nördlichen Ende.

4 I've never tried _____. I hope I don't fall into the water!

Ich habe das **Stand-up-Paddeln** noch nie ausprobiert. Ich hoffe, ich falle nicht ins Wasser!

5 The water looks _____ today. I can't wait to go in!

Das Wasser sieht **wunderschön** aus heute. Ich kann es kaum erwarten reinzugehen!

6 Jody found _____ everywhere after her trip to the beach!

Jody fand nach ihrem Strandausflug überall **Sand**!

7 For a _____ you usually have to swim, cycle and run.

Für einen **Triathlon** muss man normalerweise schwimmen, Rad fahren und laufen.

8 There were _____ _____ at the free concert.

Bei dem kostenlosen Konzert waren **zehntausende Menschen**.

9 A big _____ filled the _____ with water.

Eine große **Welle** füllte den **Gezeitentümpel** mit Wasser.

10 Al stayed at the _____ of the pool: He can't swim well.

Al blieb am Becken**rand**: Er kann nicht gut schwimmen.

11 The kids _____ the beach while their parents relaxed in the sun.

Die Kinder **erkundeten** den Strand, während ihre Eltern sich in der Sonne entspannten.

▶ Check

6 New words and phrases

▸ SB, pp. 120–121 | VOCABULARY p. 252

1 Your _____ looks great with those jeans!

Deine **Strickjacke** sieht toll aus zu der Jeans!

2 If you don't wear an _____, your shirt will get dirty.

Wenn Sie keine **Schürze** tragen, wird Ihr Hemd schmutzig.

3 Liam often wears old-fashioned _____.

Liam trägt oft altmodische **Westen**.

4 I like to watch _____ but I can't even stand on my hands.

Ich schaue mir gern **Gymnastik** an, aber ich selbst kann nicht einmal einen Handstand.

5 Look at that _____. He's amazing!

Schau dir den **Turner** an. Er ist großartig!

6 _____ at your new school?

Wie geht's an der neuen Schule?

7 Crossword puzzle

Write the word for each picture in the crossword.

8 New words and phrases

▶ SB, p. 122 | VOCABULARY pp. 252–253

1 Write your own _____ for this photo.

Formuliere eine **Bildunterschrift** für dieses Foto.

2 Ben _____ several cameras in his father's shop. The _____ didn't take very long.

Ben **installierte** einige Kameras in dem Laden seines Vaters. Der **Einbau** hat nicht sehr lange gedauert.

3 Can I _____ my phone here? I have my own _____ with me.

Kann ich mein Handy hier **aufladen**? Ich habe mein eigenes **Ladegerät** dabei.

4 Don't _____ on this spot! It hurts!

Drück nicht auf diese Stelle! Das tut weh!

5 Do I need to _____ left or right?

Muss ich links oder rechts **wischen**?

6 You have to _____ this icon to open the app.

Du musst auf dieses Icon **tippen**, um die App zu öffnen.

7 I'm not allowed to use any electronic _____ after 10 p.m.

Ich darf nach 22 Uhr keine elektronischen **Geräte** mehr benutzen.

8 What happens if I press this _____?

Was passiert, wenn ich diese **Taste** drücke?

9 What's the name of the _____ that you need?

Wie heißt die **Textdatei**, die du brauchst?

9 Categories

Write three words from the box for each category. Careful: There are three extra words!

> apron • cardigan • device • edge • gymnastics • installation • key • mining • paddleboarding • rock pool • sand • theme • triathlon • waistcoat • wave

1 Things at the beach: _____ _____ _____

2 Computers: _____ _____ _____

3 Clothes: _____ _____ _____

4 Sports: _____ _____ _____

▶ Check

10 Instructions

Write the right words from the box to complete the instructions. Careful: There are three extra words!

> charge • connect • device • document • install • keyboard • press • swipe • switch on • tap

Please read this 1 _____ carefully!

2 _____ your new 3 _____

for at least 30 minutes before you use it for the first time.

4 _____ our app on your phone.

5 _____ the icon to open the app. Then

6 _____ the button[1] on the front of the device to

7 _____ it to your phone.

[1] **button** *der Knopf, die Taste*

🔊 11 Listen carefully!
07

Listen carefully to the sentences and write the right word in each gap.

1 _____ is black and makes your hands dirty.

2 You need to read the _____ to understand what's happening in the picture.

3 There's a new _____ student in my class.

4 Is this money yours or _____?

5 The _____ of my talk is the history of Wales.

6 I've _____ learned a lot about Wales!

7 Cathy lives on the _____ of town.

12 Odd word out

Underline the word in each group that doesn't go with the other words.

1 coal – helmet – mining – voice

2 melody – article – rhythm – song

3 car – boat – ship – ferry

4 paddleboarding – kayaking – swimming – biking

5 mine – his – they – yours

6 computer key – paper – mouse – screen

7 cardigan – waistcoat – shirt – shoes

8 cable car – wave – sand – rock pool

13 New words and phrases

▶ SB, p. 123 | VOCABULARY pp. 253–254

1 Those were not my _____ words. I know _____ what I said.

Das waren nicht meine **genauen** Worte. Ich weiß **genau**, was ich gesagt habe.

2 Scott likes to wear his grandfather's old _____.

Scott trägt gern die alte **Armbanduhr** seines Opas.

3 Freya will _____ her grandparents' new computer.

Freya wird den neuen Computer ihrer Großeltern **einrichten**.

4 We all _____ the new plan.

Wir **stimmten** alle dem neuen Plan **zu**.

5 Jack _____ me at five o'clock.

Jack **willigte ein**, mich um 17 Uhr **zu treffen**.

6 The boys didn't _____ but they were still friendly.

Die Jungs **stimmten mir** nicht **zu**, waren aber trotzdem freundlich.

7 We _____ a topic and then worked on our presentation together.

Wir **einigten uns auf** ein Thema und arbeiteten dann zusammen an unserer Präsentation.

8 What are the _____ for using this app?

Wie lauten die **Bedingungen** für die Verwendung dieser App?

9 I can't _____ my phone _____ the car.

Ich kann mein Handy nicht **mit** dem Auto **koppeln**.

10 Can you please _____ this document for me? I don't have a _____.

Kannst du bitte dieses Dokument für mich **ausdrucken**? Ich habe keinen **Drucker**.

11 Jane helped Alex _____ his document.

Jane hat Alex geholfen, sein Dokument **zu formatieren**.

12 Which _____ do you prefer: large or small?

Welches **Format** findest du besser: groß oder klein?

13 The answer is _____.

Die Antwort ist **einfach**.

▶ Check

14 New words and phrases

▶SB, p. 124 | VOCABULARY p. 254

1 I don't want to _____ the topic, I'm just telling you my opinion.
Ich will das Thema nicht **diskutieren**, ich sage dir einfach meine Meinung.

2 We made some very good arguments and won the _____.
Wir haben einige sehr gute Argumente vorgebracht und die **Debatte** gewonnen.

3 The game today will be boring: It's FC _____ United.
Das Spiel heute wird langweilig. Es ist FC **gegen** United.

4 Over 1,000 people _____ my _____.
Über 1.000 Leute **abonnieren** meinen **Kanal**.

5 Angie will _____ an article to you.
Angie wird dir einen Artikel **weiterleiten**.

6 I'd like to _____ if that's OK with you!
Ich würde gern **in Kontakt bleiben**, wenn das für dich okay ist.

7 My old friend _____ _____ with me again after five years.
Meine alte Freundin **hat** nach fünf Jahren wieder mit mir **Kontakt aufgenommen**.

8 We _____ when she moved.
Wir **verloren den Kontakt**, als sie umgezogen ist.

9 I liked your _____ my post.
Mir hat dein **Kommentar zu** meinem Post gut gefallen.

10 Sport is good for our _____.
Sport ist gut für unser **Wohlergehen**.

11 It isn't nice to read your sister's _____!
Es ist nicht nett, das **Tagebuch** deiner Schwester zu lesen!

15 Verbs

Tick the right verb for each definition.

1 to discuss two sides of a question — pair ☐ agree ☐ debate ☐
2 to regularly get videos, a newspaper, etc. from sb. — subscribe ☐ get in touch ☐ forward ☐
3 to read and correct a text — swipe ☐ edit ☐ format ☐
4 to put a program into a computer — tap ☐ install ☐ charge ☐
5 to go around an area in order to learn about it — explore ☐ print ☐ allow ☐

16 New words and phrases

► SB, p. 125 | VOCABULARY pp. 254–255

1 With _____ would you like to speak?   Mit **wem** möchten Sie sprechen?

2 "Hi" is an _____ greeting.   „Hi" ist eine **informelle** Begrüßung.

3 We stayed in a holiday flat _____ a hotel.   Wir wohnten in einer Ferienwohnung **statt** in einem Hotel.

4 Jamie's _____ doesn't give any personal information about him.   Jamies **Profil** enthält keine persönlichen Informationen über ihn.

5 _____ come to your house after school?   **Soll ich** nach der Schule zu dir nach Hause kommen?

6 _____. All finished!   **Hier, bitte schön**. Alles fertig!

7 _____ send you an email?   **Möchtest du, dass ich** dir eine E-Mail schicke?

17 Definitions

Read the definitions and write the word from the unit.

1 a book that you write in about your life   _____

2 to have the same opinion or plan   _____

3 a ride at a theme park   _____

4 to change a text and make it better   _____

18 Word groups

There are two words that go with each word in a box. Draw lines to connect them.

1 mediate

phone

language

happy   tap   swipe   **3** keep in touch

2 screen   watch   email   translate

clock

4 well-being   healthy   **5** time

► Check

19 New words and phrases

▶SB, pp. 126–127 | VOCABULARY pp. 255–256

1 I think _____ is horrible. Ich finde **Cybermobbing** schrecklich.

2 *The Breakfast Club* is a film *The Breakfast Club* ist ein Film, **den** ich nie
_____ I've never seen. gesehen habe.

3 Harris showed me some interesting Harris hat mir einige interessante **Statistiken**
_____ about social media. zu sozialen Medien gezeigt.

4 _____ British **Jedes fünfte** britische Kind möchte Social-Media-
children wants to be a social media influencer. Influencer/in werden.

5 Nathan was the _____ Nathan war Mobbing-**Opfer**.
of bullying.

6 Our school _____ Unsere Schule **erlaubt** uns, an besonderen
us to wear funny clothes on special days. Tagen lustige Kleidung zu tragen.

7 Erin _____ cool Erin **erfindet** coole Geräte, die ihr
devices to help with her chores. bei ihren Arbeiten im Haushalt
helfen.

8 Dad knows someone who was in Papa kennt jemanden, der fünf
_____ for five years. Jahre im **Gefängnis** war.

9 Ellie and I had a very _____ Ellie und ich hatten eine sehr **emotionale**
discussion. Diskussion.

10 Millie has a large _____ Millie hat ein großes **Netzwerk** von Freunden
of friends but they're not the und Freundinnen, aber sie sind nicht die **Art**
_____ people that I like. **von** Leuten, die ich mag.

20 Homonyms

These words sound the same, but you write them differently and they have different meanings. Write the right English word for each German word.

too / two   theirs / there's   which / witch   one / won

1		3	
a auch; zu	_____	a ihrer/ihre/ihrs	_____
b zwei	_____	b Kurzform von *there is*	_____
2		**4**	
a Hexe	_____	a eins	_____
b welche(r/s)	_____	b gewonnen	_____

21 New words and phrases

▶ SB, pp. 128–130 | VOCABULARY pp. 256–257

1 I _____ quickly to see what it was about.

Ich **überflog den Text** schnell, um herauszufinden, worum es ging.

2 Friends don't _____ each other.

Freunde **lügen** sich nicht **an**.

3 You have to _____ your email address to use this website.

Man muss seine E-Mail-Adresse **eintippen**, um diese Webseite nutzen zu können.

4 I like pizza _____ pasta.

Ich mag **sowohl** Pizza **als auch** Pasta.

5 Have you heard the _____ news?

Hast du die **neuesten** Nachrichten gehört?

6 _____ ?

Wen interessiert das?

7 Please tell me the _____ .

Sag mir bitte die **Wahrheit**.

8 I _____ some really bad photos.

Ich **löschte** einige wirklich schlechte Fotos.

9 It was so cold outside that I could see my _____ .

Es war draußen so kalt, dass ich meinen **Atem** sehen konnte.

10 Our dog is _____ _____ the new baby.

Unser Hund ist **eifersüchtig auf** das neue Baby.

11 She's _____ here _____ name I know.

Sie ist **die einzige Person** hier, **deren** Namen ich kenne.

12 Please listen to me _____ !

Hör mir bitte **dieses eine Mal** zu!

13 Is this the right _____ to repair the radio?

Ist das hier das richtige **Werkzeug**, um das Radio zu reparieren?

14 The _____ isn't very good in this room.

Die **Beleuchtung** ist nicht sehr gut in diesem Raum.

22 Find the mistakes

There is one MISTAKE in each sentence. Underline and correct it.

1 We took a cabel car to the top of a mountain in Wales yesterday. _____

2 It's very popular: Tens of thausends of people travel on it every year. _____

3 It was cold at the top of the mountain but we had an exzellent view of the city! _____

4 Everyone had a lovly time and we stayed up there for hours. _____

23 New words and phrases

► SB, p. 131 | VOCABULARY p. 257

1 I watch more _____ than films.

Ich sehe mehr **Serien** als Filme.

2 Daniel _____ his own clothes.

Daniel **näht** seine eigene Kleidung.

3 My _____ looks very red: too much sun!

Meine **Haut** sieht sehr rot aus: zu viel Sonne!

4 That _____ looks really good on you!

Der **Kopfschmuck** steht dir wirklich gut!

24 New words and phrases

► SB, p. 132 | VOCABULARY pp. 257–258

1 The traffic is _____ well this morning.

Der Verkehr **fließt** heute Morgen gut.

2 What does this _____ mean?

Was bedeutet dieses **Symbol**?

3 You can use _____ instead of the whole words.

Sie können **Abkürzungen** statt ganzer Wörter verwenden.

4 Try to _____ your thoughts before you start writing.

Versuch mal, deine Gedanken zu **ordnen**, bevor du anfängst zu schreiben.

5 What's your worst _____ ?

Was ist deine schlechteste **Angewohnheit**?

6 I like to enjoy the weekend without a lot of homework _____ .

Ich genieße gern das Wochenende ohne großen Hausaufgaben**stress**.

7 Roxy _____ me because I wrote a negative comment about her hamster.

Roxy **hat** mich **geblockt**, weil ich einen negativen Kommentar zu ihrem Hamster geschrieben habe.

8 Please _____ your talk in three sentences.

Fass bitte deinen Vortrag in drei Sätzen **zusammen**.

9 _____ , I want to say thank you.

Zunächst einmal möchte ich mich bedanken.

25 New words and phrases

▶ SB, p. 133 | VOCABULARY p. 258

1 Where did you find this _____?
   Please give us the _____.

   Wo hast du diese **Abbildung** gefunden? Nenn uns bitte die **Quelle**.

2 Rex _____ to tell us a very long story.

   Rex **fing an**, uns eine sehr lange Geschichte zu erzählen.

3 You can _____ the change.

   Du kannst das Wechselgeld **behalten**.

4 The baby _____ in his bed and slept.

   Das Baby **lag** in seinem Bettchen und schlief.

5 I _____ never _____ clothes before.

   Ich **habe** noch nie Kleidung **genäht**.

26 The fourth word

Write the missing word.

1 swimmer – swimming →   gymnast – _____

2 fake – real →   a lie – _____

3 (to) connect – connection →   (to) breathe – _____

4 I – mine →   we – _____

5 she – hers →   they – _____

6 food – (to) cook →   clothes – _____

7 song – (to) listen to →   image – _____

🔊 27 Listen carefully!
08

Listen carefully to the sentences and write the right word in each gap.

1 My sister was the _____ of a really mean kid in her class.

2 _____ was a big problem at her school, but it's much better now.

3 John uses too many _____ in his texts. I don't understand them!

4 I'm very _____ of people who can sew!

5 This jacket has _____ here for months. I don't wear it because I can't repair it.

6 _____ apple is this?

▶ Check ⮐

28 Let's talk: Hilfe anbieten, erbitten und annehmen – ein Telefongespräch führen

Complete the telephone conversation.   ▶ SB, p. 211 and p. 212

Hi! It's me, Peter!

1 _____

_____

Begrüße Peter und frage ihn, wie es so geht.

Great, thanks. Listen, I need some help. I'd like to use social media. But I don't know where to start. I know you use a lot of social media.

2 *That's right!* _____

_____

Biete deine Hilfe an.

3 _____

_____

_____

_____

Thanks! Can you help me make some accounts?

Bejahe und frage Peter, ob du ihm das an seinem Handy zeigen sollst.

That would be great, thanks!

4 _____

_____

Frag ihn, ob er später Zeit hat.

5 _____

_____

Sag Peter, dass du ihn nicht hören kannst. Die Verbindung ist schlecht.

Can you hear me now?

Yes, I can hear you.

I said, yes, I'm free later. Can we meet at my house in an hour?

6 _____

_____

Sage zu und verabschiede dich.

Unit 5
Two Irelands: Together

1 New words and phrases

SB, pp. 148–149 | VOCABULARY pp. 258–259

1	Most people in the Republic of Ireland are _____; only about 4% are _____.	Die meisten Menschen in der Republik Irland sind **katholisch**; nur etwa 4 % sind **protestantisch**.
2	British _____ in Northern Ireland began in the 1600s.	Die britische **Herrschaft** in Nordirland begann im 17. Jahrhundert.
3	_____ were a terrible time in Ireland's history. There were _____ with soldiers.	**Der Nordirlandkonflikt** war eine schreckliche Zeit in Irlands Geschichte. Es gab **Kontrollpunkte** mit Soldaten.
4	We stayed at a nice _____ in Belfast.	Wir wohnten in einer netten **Frühstückspension** in Belfast.
5	Can you _____ a good film about the history of Ireland?	Kannst du einen guten Film über die Geschichte Irlands **empfehlen**?

2 New words and phrases

SB, p. 150 | VOCABULARY pp. 259–260

1	I've never been _____, so I don't have a _____.	Ich war noch nie **im Ausland**, daher habe ich keinen **Reisepass**.
2	If you want to travel in the EU, you just need an _____.	Wenn man in der EU reisen möchte, braucht man nur einen **Personalausweis**.
3	At what _____ can you drive a car in Ireland?	Ab welchem **Alter** darf man in Irland Auto fahren?
4	This course is for _____ learners.	Dieser Kurs ist für **fortgeschrittene** Lernende.
5	Our _____ in Belfast was clean and comfortable.	Unsere **Unterkunft** in Belfast war sauber und gemütlich.
6	Is the water in the _____ boiling?	Kocht das Wasser in dem **Wasserkocher**?
7	This ring _____ James.	Dieser Ring **gehört** James.

3 New words and phrases

▶ SB, p. 151 | VOCABULARY p. 260

1 My brother and I share a room with

   _____ .

   Mein Bruder und ich teilen uns ein Zimmer mit **zwei einzelnen Betten**.

2 We always stay in hotels that offer a

   _____ .

   Wir übernachten immer in Hotels, die ein **warmes Frühstück** anbieten.

3 There were a lot of _____ at breakfast this morning.

   Heute Morgen waren viele **Gäste** beim Frühstück.

4 The breakfast _____ is amazing! They have _____ ,

   _____ , fruit

   and a lot more!

   Das Frühstücks**büfett** ist großartig! Sie haben **Getreideflocken**, **Aufschnitt**, Obst und vieles mehr!

5 Should I complete the _____ or do you want to do it?

   Soll ich das **Formular** ausfüllen oder willst du es machen?

4 New words and phrases

▶ SB, p. 152 | VOCABULARY pp. 260–261

1 This book _____ the history of Northern Ireland.

   Dieses Buch **befasst sich mit** der Geschichte Nordirlands.

2 Ezra likes to read books by authors _____ Veronica Roth.

   Ezra liest gern Bücher von Autorinnen **wie** Veronica Roth.

3 I don't really like the _____ in this hotel.

   Mir gefallen die **Kunstwerke** in diesem Hotel nicht so richtig.

4 The city is going to _____ _____ that ugly building.

   Die Stadt wird das hässliche Gebäude **abreißen**.

5 We can _____ the sights and visit three today and three tomorrow. Which _____ are you most interested in?

   Wir können uns die Sehenswürdigkeiten **einteilen** und heute drei und morgen drei besuchen. Welche **Attraktion** interessiert dich am meisten?

5 How do you spell it?

Tick the box with the right spelling.

1 A (to) recommend ☐
   B (to) reccomend ☐
   C (to) recomend ☐

2 A accomodation ☐
   B accommodation ☐
   C acomodation ☐

3 A buffet ☐
   B bufett ☐
   C bufet ☐

4 A kettel ☐
   B ketle ☐
   C kettle ☐

5 A cereals ☐
   B sereals ☐
   C cerials ☐

6 A delt ☐
   B dellt ☐
   C dealt ☐

7 A cold meet ☐
   B cold meat ☐
   C could meat ☐

8 A brekfest ☐
   B breakfast ☐
   C breckfast ☐

9 A geusst ☐
   B gest ☐
   C guest ☐

6 A review of The Beyond B&B

Complete the review with the words from the box. Careful: There are three extra words!

> artwork • bath • bed and breakfast • buffet • cereals • cold meats • cooked breakfast • divide up • guests • kettle • recommend • take down • twin beds

Review by AnnieL from London, November 2024

★★★★★

I stayed at this cute 1 _____ with my friend last week and we loved it. We 2 _____ it to anyone who is going to Belfast. The room had 3 _____, which were very comfortable and we slept well each night. There was a 4 _____ in our room, so we had hot tea there every afternoon. In the morning, Earl and Jack serve a delicious 5 _____ _____ for their 6 _____. On Sundays they have a big breakfast 7 _____ with 8 _____, fruit, cheese and several different kinds of 9 _____, such as salami. The 10 _____ was large and clean, and there was always enough hot water! The Beyond B&B was really a great place to stay.

► Check

7 Travel ABC

Look at pages 149 to 151 and complete the travel ABC.

ab ___ ___ ___ ___	journey	sight
bed and ___ ___ ___ ___ ___ ___ ___ ___	k ___ ___ ___ ___	t ___ ___ ___ beds
ch ___ ___ ___ ___ ___ ___ ___ ___	landscape	underground
destination	map	visit
experience	national	walk
f ___ ___ ___	official language	Brex ___ ___
g ___ ___ ___ ___	p ___ ___ ___ ___ ___ ___ ___	country
hotel	queue	zoo
i ___ ___ ___ ___ ___ ___ ___ card	r ___ ___ ___ ___ ___ ___ ___ ___	

8 Odd word out

Underline the word in each group that doesn't go with the other words.

1 Catholic – Irish – Muslim – Protestant

2 draw – paint – artwork – science

3 age – hair colour – height – name

4 B&B – checkpoint – holiday flat – hotel

5 cereals – cold meat – breakfast – pizza

6 sight – attraction – view – bed

7 form – kettle – milk – tea

8 passport – rucksack – identity card – document

9 Almost the same

Match the sentences that have similar meanings.

1 The students didn't like the way the teacher ruled the class.

2 I always recommend this book to people.

3 He goes abroad every summer.

4 Please tell me your age.

5 He has found a good accommodation.

a I tell everyone that they should read this.

b Can you tell me how old you are?

c He discovered a nice place to stay.

d The kids didn't agree with the methods in their lessons.

e In July he always visits another country.

10 New words and phrases

▶ SB, pp. 154–157 | VOCABULARY pp. 261–262

1 The _____ of this meeting is to find a solution to the problem.

Das **Ziel** dieses Treffens ist es, eine Lösung für das Problem zu finden.

2 I've practised this _____ about a hundred times.

Ich habe diese **Tanznummer** ungefähr hundert Mal geübt.

3 "I didn't see you at school today." –
"I _____ see you _____."

„Ich habe dich heute nicht in der Schule gesehen." –
„Ich **habe** dich **auch nicht** gesehen."

4 _____ with your match today! I'm sure you'll _____.

Viel Glück bei deinem Spiel heute! Ich bin mir sicher, dass du **es gut machen** wirst.

5 We _____ the other team 5:3.

Wir **schlugen** die andere Mannschaft mit 5:3.

6 I always smile when I'm _____.

Ich lächele immer, wenn ich **nervös** bin.

7 It's quite dark in here so you may need a _____.

Da es hier ziemlich dunkel ist, brauchst du vielleicht einen **Blitz**.

8 All of the questions _____ me.

Die Fragen verwirrten mich alle.

9 _____ should always be fair.

Richter/innen sollten immer fair sein.

10 I didn't break your phone _____.

Ich habe dein Handy nicht **mit Absicht** kaputt gemacht.

11 Nick has a strong sense of _____.

Nick hat einen starken Sinn für **Gerechtigkeit**.

12 Twelve _____ four is forty-eight, not forty-six.

Zwölf **mal** vier ist achtundvierzig, nicht sechsundvierzig.

13 The museum was _____!

Das Museum war **spektakulär**!

▶ Check

11 Definitions

Tick the right word for each definition.

1	to be part of something	to confuse	☐	to belong to	☐	to sum up	☐
2	to put into parts or groups	to divide up	☐	to fight	☐	to travel	☐
3	at a high level	advanced	☐	old	☐	easy	☐
4	a strong, quick light, e.g. from a camera	lamp	☐	spot	☐	flash	☐
5	the result of dealing with people fairly	judge	☐	justice	☐	kindness	☐
6	a person who decides who wins something	audience	☐	teacher	☐	judge	☐
7	to win against someone in a competition	to lose	☐	to beat	☐	to score	☐

🔊 12 Listen carefully!
09

Listen carefully to the sentences and write the right word in each gap.

1 I learned a lot about the _____ at this museum.

2 My friend _____ this restaurant to me.

3 What does _____ mean to you?

4 How are the _____ in Belfast?

5 We have _____ coming for the weekend.

6 I don't like _____ restaurants.

7 My father put three _____ on the table.

8 The _____ of the book is to give new information about the history of Belfast.

9 That film really _____ me: I didn't understand anything!

10 At your _____, my hobby was collecting rocks.

13 New words and phrases

▶ SB, p. 158 | VOCABULARY p. 262

1 You can _____ amazing images in seconds with this app.

Mit dieser App kann man innerhalb von Sekunden erstaunliche Bilder **generieren**.

2 It's very _____ in here.

Es ist sehr **hell** hier drin.

3 I like old _____ furniture.

Ich mag alte **Holz**möbel.

4 That _____ is very dirty!

Der **Teppich** ist sehr schmutzig!

5 Your sofa looks very _____.

Dein Sofa sieht sehr **gemütlich** aus.

6 We closed the _____ in our hotel room.

Wir haben die **Vorhänge** in unserem Hotel-zimmer zugezogen.

7 Don't _____ the story too much. Just enjoy it!

Analysiere die Geschichte nicht zu sehr. Genieße sie einfach!

14 New words and phrases

▶ SB, p. 159 | VOCABULARY p. 263

1 I bought this chocolate because the _____ was so funny.

Ich habe diese Schokolade gekauft, weil der **Werbespot** so lustig war.

2 What are your best _____?

Was sind deine besten **Eigenschaften**?

3 I know the vocabulary from the unit but I don't understand the _____.

Ich kann den Wortschatz aus der Unit, verstehe aber die **Grammatik** nicht.

4 Thank you for that presentation. It was very _____!

Danke für die Präsentation. Sie war sehr **informativ**.

5 We _____ their team several times.

Wir **haben** ihre Mannschaft mehrmals **besiegt**.

6 I _____ with Louise last weekend and had a great time.

Ich **hing** letztes Wochenende mit Louise **rum** und hatte eine tolle Zeit.

7 Ali _____ my money safe for me.

Ali **bewahrte** mein Geld sicher für mich **auf**.

8 I _____ never _____ the sea.

Ich **habe** das Meer noch nie **gesehen**.

▶ Check